Human Rights

Other Books of Related Interest:

Opposing Viewpoints Series

Civil Liberties

Globalization

Illegal Immigration

The Internet

Social Issues

Current Controversies Series

Civil Liberties

Civil Rights

Ethics

At Issue Series

Can Democracy Succeed in the Middle East?

Does the Internet Benefit Society?

How Should the United States Treat Prisoners of the War
 on Terrorism?

Is Torture Ever Justified?

What is the State of Human Rights?

What Rights Should Illegal Immigrants Have?

Human Rights

Adela Soliz, Book Editor

GREENHAVEN PRESS

An imprint of Thomson Gale, a part of The Thomson Corporation

Detroit • New York • San Francisco • New Haven, Conn. • Waterville, Maine • London

Christine Nasso, *Publisher*
Elizabeth Des Chenes, *Managing Editor*

For more information, contact:
Greenhaven Press
27500 Drake Rd.
Farmington Hills, MI 48331-3535
Or you can visit our Internet site at http://www.gale.com

LIBRARY OF CONGRESS CATALOGING-IN-PUBLICATION DATA

Human rights / Adela Soliz, book editor.
    p. cm. -- (Contemporary issues companion)
  Includes bibliographical references and index.
  ISBN-13: 978-0-7377-2458-5 (lib. hardcover : alk. paper)
  ISBN-10: 0-7377-2458-7 (lib. hardcover : alk. paper)
  ISBN-13: 978-0-7377-2459-2 (pbk. : alk. paper)
  ISBN-10: 0-7377-2459-5 (pbk. : alk. paper)
 1. Human rights. I. Soliz, Adela.
  JC571.H7665 2007
  323--dc22
                                      2006022903

Contents

Foreword   **9**

Introduction   **12**

Chapter 1: Defining Human Rights

1. The United Nations' Universal Declaration   **17**
   of Human Rights
   United Nations

2. The United Nations Is Changing the Way It   **26**
   Addresses Human Rights Challenges
   Julie A. Mertus

3. International Human Rights Law Has Evolved   **30**
   to Meet New Challenges
   Thomas Buergenthal

4. Islamic Reactions to Western Ideas of   **39**
   Human Rights
   Emile Sahliyeh

Chapter 2: Worldwide Examples of Human Rights Violations

1. Uzbekistan's Dictator Is Violating Human Rights   **47**
   Jonathan Freedland

2. China Is Committing Numerous Human   **52**
   Rights Violations
   Amnesty International

3. Ethnic Conflict in Sudan Is Causing Large-Scale   **59**
   Human Rights Violations
   Nsongurua J. Udombana

4. The United States Is Violating the Human Rights   **67**
   of Suspected Terrorist Prisoners
   Michael Ratner

Chapter 3: How Can Human Rights Be Protected or Improved?

1. Democracy Promotes Human Rights   77
   G. Shabbir Cheema

2. Democracy Does Not Guarantee Human Rights   85
   CNN.com

3. Globalization Promotes Human Rights   90
   Daniel Griswold

4. Suing Global Corporations Can End Their
   Human Rights Abuses   96
   Daphne Eviatar

5. The United Nations Promotes Human Rights   102
   Jerry Pubantz

6. The UN Human Rights Commission Should
   Not Admit Human Rights Violators to
   Its Membership   111
   Frida Ghitis

7. The Internet Can Help Improve Human Rights   114
   Lloyd Axworthy

Chapter 4: Personal Perspectives on Human Rights Issues

1. The Plight of Refugees from Liberia's Civil War   123
   Caroline Moorehead

2. A Former Chinese Political Prisoner Discusses
   His Detention   132
   Luke Harding

3. An Aid Worker Describes Working in Sudan
   During the Civil War   138
   "Sleepless in Sudan"

4. The Former High Commissioner for Human
   Rights Discusses Key Human Rights Concerns   145
   Mary Robinson, interviewed by Ian Williams

Organizations to Contact   **153**

Bibliography   **158**

Index   **164**

Foreword

In the news, on the streets, and in neighborhoods, individuals are confronted with a variety of social problems. Such problems may affect people directly: A young woman may struggle with depression, suspect a friend of having bulimia, or watch a loved one battle cancer. And even the issues that do not directly affect her private life—such as religious cults, domestic violence, or legalized gambling—still impact the larger society in which she lives. Discovering and analyzing the complexities of issues that encompass communal and societal realms as well as the world of personal experience is a valuable educational goal in the modern world.

Effectively addressing social problems requires familiarity with a constantly changing stream of data. Becoming well informed about today's controversies is an intricate process that often involves reading myriad primary and secondary sources, analyzing political debates, weighing various experts' opinions—even listening to firsthand accounts of those directly affected by the issue. For students and general observers, this can be a daunting task because of the sheer volume of information available in books, periodicals, on the evening news, and on the Internet. Researching the consequences of legalized gambling, for example, might entail sifting through congressional testimony on gambling's societal effects, examining private studies on Indian gaming, perusing numerous Web sites devoted to Internet betting, and reading essays written by lottery winners as well as interviews with recovering compulsive gamblers. Obtaining valuable information can be time-consuming—since it often requires researchers to pore over numerous documents and commentaries before discovering a source relevant to their particular investigation.

Greenhaven's Contemporary Issues Companion series seeks to assist this process of research by providing readers with useful and pertinent information about today's complex issues. Each volume in this anthology series focuses on a topic of current interest, presenting informative and thought-provoking selections written from a wide variety of viewpoints. The readings selected by the editors include such diverse sources as personal accounts and case studies, pertinent factual and statistical articles, and relevant commentaries and overviews. This diversity of sources and views, found in every Contemporary Issues Companion, offers readers a broad perspective in one convenient volume.

In addition, each title in the Contemporary Issues Companion series is designed especially for young adults. The selections included in every volume are chosen for their accessibility and are expertly edited in consideration of both the reading and comprehension levels of the audience. The structure of the anthologies also enhances accessibility. An introductory essay places each issue in context and provides helpful facts such as historical background or current statistics and legislation that pertain to the topic. The chapters that follow organize the material and focus on specific aspects of the book's topic. Every essay is introduced by a brief summary of its main points and biographical information about the author. These summaries aid in comprehension and can also serve to direct readers to material of immediate interest and need. Finally, a comprehensive index allows readers to efficiently scan and locate content.

The Contemporary Issues Companion series is an ideal launching point for research on a particular topic. Each anthology in the series is composed of readings taken from an extensive gamut of resources, including periodicals, newspapers, books, government documents, the publications of private and public organizations, and Internet Web sites. In these volumes, readers will find factual support suitable for use in reports, debates, speeches, and research papers. The anthologies also facilitate further research, featuring a book and periodical bibliography and a list of organizations to contact for additional information.

A perfect resource for both students and the general reader, Greenhaven's Contemporary Issues Companion series is sure to be a valued source of current, readable information on social problems that interest young adults. It is the editor's hope that readers will find the Contemporary Issues Companion series useful as a starting point to formulate their own opinions about and answers to the complex issues of the present day.

Introduction

Human rights standards were first adopted on a global basis when the United Nations drafted the Universal Declaration of Human Rights in 1948. The Universal Declaration established a variety of rights that are inherent to all people in all nations, such as the right to education and freedom from torture and wrongful imprisonment. The member nations of the United Nations were and still are obliged to uphold these rights, and watchdog groups such as Amnesty International (founded in 1961) and Human Rights Watch (founded in 1978) monitor states' attention to these laws. Failure to adhere to the Universal Declaration could at best bring about exposure and negative publicity, or at worst, UN sanctions.

Since the adoption of the Universal Declaration of Human Rights, however, the UN's focus has increasingly shifted from a concern with abusive nation-states to a concern with international relationships and global politics. Human rights, today, have as much to do with curbing the power of international corporations as they have to do with curbing the power of dictators. The influence of international or multinational corporations—tacitly supported by their respective governments—has also brought attention to the fact that many liberal democracies, while cherishing above-average human rights standards at home, have poor records when it comes to their interests overseas.

The United States, for example, has always been a staunch defender of human rights, yet critics charge that its international politics and trade practices have resulted in a loss of legitimacy. In recent years the accusations have been leveled at the administration of George W. Bush, which supposedly has sought greater economic and strategic ties with abusive foreign governments and therefore lessened pressure on them to embrace democracy. In a May 2006 article, the *Global Infor-*

mation Network writes that "the Bush administration has pretty much dropped its democratic pretenses in favor of stability—and the 'friendly' autocrats who can provide it, especially those with plentiful oil and gas resources and strategically placed real estate vis-à-vis emerging foes." Besides its global preoccupations, the United States is also facing criticism for human rights abuses at home. Strict immigration policies and the questionable treatment of prisoners captured in the ongoing war against terrorism are two of the salient issues that have damaged the U.S. reputation both at home and abroad. Some critics have even charged that because the United States did not even vie for a seat on the UN Human Rights Council in 2006, concern for human rights is no longer a prime interest of the government.

Nations with struggling economies, however, still look to improved human rights as a means to build stronger foreign ties. Turkey, for example, has suffered from charges of human rights abuse that has kept it from enjoying widespread trade. The government of Turkey's prime minister Recep Tayyip Erdogan is attempting to change the record. Reports of Eastern European countries' bids to join the European Union also suggest that a nation's legitimacy is increasingly tied to its human rights record. Erdogan hopes that by granting more liberal reforms, his country might join the European Union (EU), and some believe his plan may be working. In September 2004 the *Economist* newsmagazine wrote:

> In the past, [Turkey] has suffered from plenty of failings, ranging from political and economic instability, to the interfering role of its army, to a record of human-rights abuses. These made it easy for the Europeans to fob off previous Turkish bids to join. But over the past two years, the government of Recep Tayyip Erdogan's Justice and Development party has enacted a swathe of reforms, in the hope of meeting the "Copenhagen criteria" that govern eligibility to join the EU.

The reforms alluded to are not economic reforms, but rather reforms that push Turkey closer to liberal democracy. Turkey's economy is only a third of the size of the average country in the European Union, yet the possibility of moving Turkey toward liberal democracy and increasing human rights, particularly because of its proximity to the Middle East, prompts observers to believe that the European Union is likely to admit Turkey despite its economic weakness.

Human rights also figure prominently in discussions of China's entrance into the world market. Experts suggest that because China has become an economic powerhouse, the government must begin to clean up its human rights record. Much of China's economic strength has for decades been tied to sweatshops and ambivalence toward the rights of its labor force. This has given it the power to undercut local trade in both strong economies and in the poorest of nations. As the *Economist* noted in November 2005, "[China's] indifference to human rights has given its companies an edge in places as disparate as Uzbekistan, Zimbabwe, Sudan and Iran." What remains unsure, however, is whether China's inexpensive manufacturing will convince the world that its human rights violations can be ignored. Unlike Turkey, China has the economic muscle to influence world trade without tending to human rights complaints. The voices of Amnesty International and Human Rights Watch, however, are strong and do carry international clout. Whether the call to liberal reform will trump economics in China's international relations is yet to be seen.

While human rights are increasingly the grounds on which a nation's legitimacy is judged, few observers have agreed on how best to promote human rights. The United Nations has been accused of being partisan in calling human rights abusers to task. For example, the United Nations Human Rights Commission has been discredited because so many of its members are themselves notorious human rights abusers. Reporting on the creation of a new Human Rights Council in 2006 the *New York Times* writes, "The previous commission was long a public embarrassment to the United Nations because countries like Sudan, Libya and Zimbabwe became members and thereby thwarted the investigation of their own human rights records." Similarly, the Western ideal of promoting democracy has also been shaded as favoritism for those developing nations willing to bend to Western economic plans and political agendas. Many critics debate the notion that democracy is necessarily a guarantor of human rights. "Despite their democratically elected governments," a 2006 CNN report maintains, "countries such as Venezuela and Russia do not always respect democratic principles such as human rights."

While critics harp on such flaws, however, the United Nations and the promotion of liberal democracy remain two bastions in the global effort to improve human rights. Whether these forces are the best the world can offer is still a contentious issue, and it is one taken up by the authors within *Contemporary Issues Companion: Human Rights*. Other commentators in this anthology address how human rights are defined, how they have been abused, and how they can be protected. The book also includes valuable firsthand accounts of human rights violations and solutions, elevating the drama of the human rights debate to a less abstract and more personal level.

CHAPTER 1

Defining Human Rights

The United Nations' Universal Declaration of Human Rights

United Nations

The following selection is the preamble and thirty articles that constitute the Universal Declaration of Human Rights, which the United Nations General Assembly adopted in December 1948. The Universal Declaration of Human Rights was created in response to the crimes against humanity perpetrated during World War II. Human rights theorists and organizations that fight to protect human rights have adhered to the declaration when defining human rights. One essential idea proclaimed by the declaration is that human rights are universal. This means that they span national borders and trump national law. The declaration describes each right that the United Nations considers to be universal. It lays out rights belonging to all individuals, including rights to privacy, education, protection against wrongful imprisonment, and employment.

The United Nations was created in 1945 to maintain international peace and security by promoting cooperation and friendly relations among nations. Today the Office of the High Commissioner for Human Rights is mandated by the United Nations Secretariat to promote and protect, for all people, the rights set down in the Universal Declaration of Human Rights.

Preamble

Whereas recognition of the inherent dignity and of the equal and inalienable rights of all members of the human family is the foundation of freedom, justice and peace in the world,

Whereas disregard and contempt for human rights have resulted in barbarous acts which have outraged the conscience

United Nations, "Universal Declaration of Human Rights," 1948. © 1948 United Nations. Reprinted with the permission of the United Nations.

of mankind, and the advent of a world in which human beings shall enjoy freedom of speech and belief and freedom from fear and want has been proclaimed as the highest aspiration of the common people,

Whereas it is essential, if man is not to be compelled to have recourse, as a last resort, to rebellion against tyranny and oppression, that human rights should be protected by the rule of law,

Whereas it is essential to promote the development of friendly relations between nations,

Whereas the peoples of the United Nations have in the Charter [that created the United Nations in 1945] reaffirmed their faith in fundamental human rights, in the dignity and worth of the human person and in the equal rights of men and women and have determined to promote social progress and better standards of life in larger freedom,

Whereas Member States have pledged themselves to achieve, in cooperation with the United Nations, the promotion of universal respect for and observance of human rights and fundamental freedoms,

Whereas a common understanding of these rights and freedoms is of the greatest importance for the full realization of this pledge,

Now, therefore,

The General Assembly,

Proclaims this Universal Declaration of Human Rights as a common standard of achievement for all peoples and all nations, to the end that every individual and every organ of society, keeping this Declaration constantly in mind, shall strive by teaching and education to promote respect for these rights and freedoms and by progressive measures, national and international, to secure their universal and effective recognition and observance, both among the peoples of Member States themselves and among the peoples of territories under their jurisdiction.

Article 1

All human beings are born free and equal in dignity and rights. They are endowed with reason and conscience and should act towards one another in a spirit of brotherhood.

Article 2

Everyone is entitled to all the rights and freedoms set forth in this Declaration, without distinction of any kind, such as race, colour, sex, language, religion, political or other opinion, national or social origin, property, birth or other status. Furthermore, no distinction shall be made on the basis of the political, jurisdictional or international status of the country or territory to which a person belongs, whether it be independent, trust, non-self-governing or under any other limitation of sovereignty.

Article 3

Everyone has the right to life, liberty and security of person.

Article 4

No one shall be held in slavery or servitude; slavery and the slave trade shall be prohibited in all their forms.

Article 5

No one shall be subjected to torture or to cruel, inhuman or degrading treatment or punishment.

Article 6

Everyone has the right to recognition everywhere as a person before the law.

Article 7

All are equal before the law and are entitled without any discrimination to equal protection of the law. All are entitled to equal protection against any discrimination in violation of this Declaration and against any incitement to such discrimination.

Article 8

Everyone has the right to an effective remedy by the competent national tribunals for acts violating the fundamental rights granted him by the constitution or by law.

Article 9

No one shall be subjected to arbitrary arrest, detention or exile.

Article 10

Everyone is entitled in full equality to a fair and public hearing by an independent and impartial tribunal, in the determination of his rights and obligations and of any criminal charge against him.

Article 11

1. Everyone charged with a penal offence has the right to be presumed innocent until proved guilty according to law in a public trial at which he has had all the guarantees necessary for his defence.

2. No one shall be held guilty of any penal offence on account of any act or omission which did not constitute a penal offence, under national or international law, at the time when it was committed. Nor shall a heavier penalty be imposed than the one that was applicable at the time the penal offence was committed.

Article 12

No one shall be subjected to arbitrary interference with his privacy, family, home or correspondence, nor to attacks upon his honour and reputation. Everyone has the right to the protection of the law against such interference or attacks.

Article 13

1. Everyone has the right to freedom of movement and residence within the borders of each State.

2. Everyone has the right to leave any country, including his own, and to return to his country.

Article 14

1. Everyone has the right to seek and to enjoy in other countries asylum from persecution.
2. This right may not be invoked in the case of prosecutions genuinely arising from non-political crimes or from acts contrary to the purposes and principles of the United Nations.

Article 15

1. Everyone has the right to a nationality.
2. No one shall be arbitrarily deprived of his nationality nor denied the right to change his nationality.

Article 16

1. Men and women of full age, without any limitation due to race, nationality or religion, have the right to marry and to found a family. They are entitled to equal rights as to marriage, during marriage and at its dissolution.
2. Marriage shall be entered into only with the free and full consent of the intending spouses.
3. The family is the natural and fundamental group unit of society and is entitled to protection by society and the State.

Article 17

1. Everyone has the right to own property alone as well as in association with others.
2. No one shall be arbitrarily deprived of his property.

Article 18

Everyone has the right to freedom of thought, conscience and religion; this right includes freedom to change his religion or belief, and freedom, either alone or in community with others and in public or private, to manifest his religion or belief in teaching, practice, worship and observance.

Article 19

Everyone has the right to freedom of opinion and expression; this right includes freedom to hold opinions without interference and to seek, receive and impart information and ideas through any media and regardless of frontiers.

Article 20

1. Everyone has the right to freedom of peaceful assembly and association.
2. No one may be compelled to belong to an association.

Article 21

1. Everyone has the right to take part in the government of his country, directly or through freely chosen representatives.
2. Everyone has the right to equal access to public service in his country.
3. The will of the people shall be the basis of the authority of government; this will shall be expressed in periodic and genuine elections which shall be by universal and equal suffrage and shall be held by secret vote or by equivalent free voting procedures.

Article 22

Everyone, as a member of society, has the right to social security and is entitled to realization, through national effort and international co-operation and in accordance with the organization and resources of each State, of the economic, social and cultural rights indispensable for his dignity and the free development of his personality.

Article 23

1. Everyone has the right to work, to free choice of employment, to just and favourable conditions of work and to protection against unemployment.

2. Everyone, without any discrimination, has the right to equal pay for equal work.

3. Everyone who works has the right to just and favourable remuneration ensuring for himself and his family an existence worthy of human dignity, and supplemented, if necessary, by other means of social protection.

4. Everyone has the right to form and to join trade unions for the protection of his interests.

Article 24

Everyone has the right to rest and leisure, including reasonable limitation of working hours and periodic holidays with pay.

Article 25

1. Everyone has the right to a standard of living adequate for the health and well-being of himself and of his family, including food, clothing, housing and medical care and necessary social services, and the right to security in the event of unemployment, sickness, disability, widowhood, old age or other lack of livelihood in circumstances beyond his control.

2. Motherhood and childhood are entitled to special care and assistance. All children, whether born in or out of wedlock, shall enjoy the same social protection.

Article 26

1. Everyone has the right to education. Education shall be free, at least in the elementary and fundamental stages. Elementary education shall be compulsory. Technical

and professional education shall be made generally available and higher education shall be equally accessible to all on the basis of merit.

2. Education shall be directed to the full development of the human personality and to the strengthening of respect for human rights and fundamental freedoms. It shall promote understanding, tolerance and friendship among all nations, racial or religious groups, and shall further the activities of the United Nations for the maintenance of peace.

3. Parents have a prior right to choose the kind of education that shall be given to their children.

Article 27

1. Everyone has the right freely to participate in the cultural life of the community, to enjoy the arts and to share in scientific advancement and its benefits.

2. Everyone has the right to the protection of the moral and material interests resulting from any scientific, literary or artistic production of which he is the author.

Article 28

Everyone is entitled to a social and international order in which the rights and freedoms set forth in this Declaration can be fully realized.

Article 29

1. Everyone has duties to the community in which alone the free and full development of his personality is possible.

2. In the exercise of his rights and freedoms, everyone shall be subject only to such limitations as are determined by law solely for the purpose of securing due recognition and respect for the rights and freedoms of

others and of meeting the just requirements of morality, public order and the general welfare in a democratic society.

3. These rights and freedoms may in no case be exercised contrary to the purposes and principles of the United Nations.

Article 30

Nothing in this Declaration may be interpreted as implying for any State, group or person any right to engage in any activity or to perform any act aimed at the destruction of any of the rights and freedoms set forth herein.

The United Nations Is Changing the Way It Addresses Human Rights Challenges

Julie A. Mertus

In the following excerpt from her book The United Nations and Human Rights: A Guide for a New Era, *Julie Mertus explains that the United Nations human rights system is broadening its mandate, or authority. The United Nations has changed its focus from setting standards for nations to follow when drafting their own human rights laws, to assisting in the enforcement of international human rights policy. For example, Mertus writes that the United Nations is taking on in-country development projects such as electoral assistance and human rights education programs for police officers. Mertus explains that development organizations, including the United Nations Development Programme, are beginning to integrate human rights into their economic and social development projects. Additionally, the United Nations is making a new effort to hold nonstate actors, such as paramilitary troops and transnational corporations responsible for human rights violations.*

Julie Mertus is associate professor and codirector of the master's program in ethics, peace and global affairs at the School of International Service at American University in Washington, D.C. She has written many articles and books, including Human Rights and Conflict *and* Kosovo: How Myths and Truths Started a War.

The evolving content of human rights, the growing diversity of actors in the UN human rights system and the

Julie A. Mertus, *The United Nations and Human Rights: A Guide for a New Era.* Andover, Hampshire: Routledge, 2005. © 2005 Julie A. Mertus. All rights reserved. Reproduced by permission of Taylor & Francis Books, U.K.

changing nature of human rights practice reflect a shift in the way in which the UN human rights system has tended to address human rights challenges.

What Is the New UN Human Rights Practice?

Nearly all guides to UN human rights practice focus on the work of UN treaty and Charter-based bodies and procedures. According to these models, monitoring and reporting of violations of civil and political rights occupy the central field of advocacy practice for the international human rights movement. New issue areas do arise, but they "are either ushered into the methodological fold of the mainstream movement, or face obstacles to their integration." . . .

Human rights complaint procedures and reporting under the treaty and Charter-based bodies remain important for human rights enforcement. Marginalized groups seeking the imprimatur of legitimacy within the mainstream human rights community continue to push for new treaties reflecting their concerns. In many respects, US standard-setting remains a crucial concern, especially for those who have not yet had input into the process. To a large extent, however, the UN human rights system has in fact moved from standard-setting to implementation of human rights policies through institutionalization and enforcement. Many of these new measures are controversial and will continue to be contested as the precise content of UN human rights practice evolves over time.

In addition to making treaties more effective, UN human rights practice today is taking on a broader mandate. Human rights practice is likely to address human rights education programs for police officers and soldiers, projects to combat trafficking in women, efforts to limit the use of child soldiers, electoral assistance, and other field-oriented, in-country endeavors. Contemporary UN human rights practice speaks to concerns once deemed to be the province of other fields, such as development, humanitarian and refugee affairs, trade, labor or security. In exceptional cases, the UN also has indicated a willingness to sanction the use of military force to address human rights violations. Vigorous human rights enforcement would not have been possible during the Cold War.

Efforts to promote human rights-based advancement of economic and social development have also received particular attention in the post-September 11 [2001] climate. In the past, development organizations often sacrificed human rights in the name of development, in an "instrumentalist *quid-pro-quo* [reciprocity] that saw human rights as a deferrable luxury of rich countries." Today, however, many development organizations—including the United Nations Development Programme (UNDP)—have publicly embraced the integration of human rights in their work, often with the explicit goal of addressing the underlying tensions that provide fertile ground for terrorist acts. At the same time, some states have reacted to September 11 by retrenching and regressing on human rights, violating the civil liberties of their citizens of Middle Eastern ancestry, torturing Afghan and Iraqi prisoners under the purported cloak of human rights, and threatening journalists with arrest should they reveal their sources in cases that would ordinarily attract little attention.

These developments have been accompanied by new attempts to hold non-state actors, including paramilitary troops, NATO [North Atlantic Treaty Organization] forces and transnational corporations, accountable for human rights abuses. The foundational international instruments of the international human rights framework, namely the Universal Declaration of Human Rights, the International Covenant on Civil and Political Rights, and the International Covenant on Economic, Social and Cultural Rights focus on the need to protect individuals from abuse by state authorities. Moreover, although these documents ostensibly place all civil and political rights (such as the right to a fair trial and freedom from torture) on an equal footing with economic, social and cultural rights (such as the right to education or health care), greater attention has been paid by most Western governments and NGOs [non-governmental organizations] to civil and political rights. This orientation has been reconsidered in recent years with an increasing realization that non-state actors, groups and organizations can also be responsible for atrocities and that economic wrongs may be as grave and as in need of redress as civil and political abuses committed by state actors. . . .

Where Does UN Human Rights Work Happen?

The answer to this question used to be easy. Simply put, UN human rights practice used to happen where the name plate on the door said "human rights." So, human rights were almost entirely contained within a limited set of specific human rights bodies. This is no longer the case. Today, virtually all United Nations bodies and specialized agencies, including the World Bank and the International Monetary Fund [two international lending institutions], are undertaking efforts to incorporate the promotion or protection of human rights into their programs and activities. To be sure, these endeavors invite criticism. For starters, many of the employees of these organizations that are confronting new human rights mandates have limited training on human rights. Nonetheless, one could argue, by bringing their own experiences and perspectives to bear on human rights problems, they offer the possibility for new solutions. . . . Human rights are currently becoming diffused throughout the UN system. Pockets still exist in which human rights can be ignored, but progress has been made nonetheless.

International Human Rights Law Has Evolved to Meet New Challenges

Thomas Buergenthal

In the following excerpt taken from the anthology Human Rights: Concept and Standards, *Thomas Buergenthal traces the development of international human rights law. International human rights law relates to infractions of human rights as defined by the United Nations' Universal Declaration of Human Rights (adopted in 1948). Buergenthal explains some of the history of international human rights law and its evolution. He states that, historically, nations have been held accountable for human rights violations. Since the 1990s, however, the UN has expanded its view of violators to include individuals and organizations, not just states. This shift in focus came about, Buergenthal claims, because the international community recognized that some states were too weak to oppose groups or individuals responsible for human rights violations within the state. Another contemporary emphasis of international human rights law that he describes is a renewed interest within the international community in protecting the rights of national, racial, ethnic, linguistic, and religious minorities because intolerance and persecution are on the rise. Finally, Buergenthal notes the greater readiness of the UN Security Council to intervene in situations of large-scale human rights violations. Since March 2000 Thomas Buergenthal has been the U.S. member of the International Court of Justice, the principal judicial structure of the United Nations. He has worked as professor of law at American University, Emory University, and other institutions. He is also the author of numerous books and articles on international human rights.*

The evolution of international human rights law cannot be conceptually divorced from the much older domestic constitutional law norms intended to safeguard the rights of the individual against arbitrary state action. As a matter of fact, much of substantive international human rights law, namely the nature or contents of these rights, has its conceptual source in the principles of domestic constitutional law embodied in the fundamental laws of various countries. Their historical and philosophical origins can, in turn, be traced back to such great milestones of human freedom as the American Declaration of Independence and the French Declaration of the Rights of Man and of the Citizen, among others. These instruments, and the national constitutions which inspired them, greatly influenced the contents of much of modern international human rights law. One cannot, for example, read Article 1 of the Universal Declaration of Human Rights, 'All human beings are born free and equal in dignity and rights', without recognizing the debt this formulation owes to the American and French Declarations and to the idea of human freedom they articulate.

The Charter of the United Nations

The modern international human rights revolution begins with the adoption of the Charter of the United Nations. While it is certainly true that international law recognized some forms of international human rights protection prior to the Charter, the process which ushered in 'the internationalization of human rights and the humanization of international law', as it has been characterized elsewhere begins with the establishment of the United Nations. The result has been a worldwide movement in which states, intergovernmental and non-governmental organizations are the principal players in a continuing struggle concerning the role the international community should play in promoting and protecting human rights.

The idea that the protection of human rights knows no international boundaries, and that the international community has an obligation to ensure that governments guarantee and protect human rights wherever they may be violated, has gradually captured the imagination of mankind. The end of the Cold War has deideologized the struggle for human rights and reinforced the international human rights movement. Today, violators of human rights can no longer count on one or the other superpower to shield them from international condemnation, a practice which in the past had a very detrimental effect on the development and application of human rights law.

This is not to say that massive violations of human rights are no longer being committed, or that the international institutions designed to prevent such violations are all in place and working effectively. Many governments still violate human rights on a large scale and many more would prefer never to have to account for their actions. But the fact is that they are increasingly being forced by a variety of external and internal factors to answer for their behaviour to the international community. This reality limits their freedom of action, and in many, albeit not all, cases contributes to an improved human rights situation. . . .

A Shift from Governmental to Personal Responsibility

International human rights law has traditionally focused on the responsibility of governments, rather than that of individuals, for violations of human rights. The assumption here was that governments have a duty not only not to violate human rights, but also to control all activities taking place within their territory, to punish human rights violations and to ensure that its own officials do not violate human rights. Although the war crimes trials following the Second World War, the Geneva Conventions on humanitarian law, and some international human rights treaties, notably the Genocide Convention, established individual international criminal responsibility for some of the most egregious violations of human rights, including genocide, crimes against humanity and war crimes, international human rights law and efforts to enforce it have for the most part focused on the behaviour and obligations of governments.

This focus has shifted to some extent in recent years. For one thing, it has become increasingly clear that some governments are simply not able to protect those within their jurisdiction from violations of human rights committed by powerful groups within the state. This has been true of terrorist groups, criminal organizations and, in certain countries, the military establishment and its allies operating outside the sphere of civilian control. Here the watchword is impunity; that is, individuals belonging to these groups have in certain countries been able to commit large-scale violations of human rights while enjoying a *de facto* [true] immunity from prosecution for what, in theory at least, are criminal acts under the law of the state where these acts are committed. It is obvious, therefore, that potential violators will not be deterred from engaging in massive human rights abuses if they know that they will always enjoy domestic impunity and that, at most, only the state will be held internationally responsible for their acts.

These realities are increasingly forcing the international community to explore ways, not only to hold the state responsible, but also to act directly against individuals the state is too weak or unwilling to punish. While various principles of international criminal law have theoretically always permitted the imposition of individual responsibility for international crimes, including some grave violations of human rights, no international tribunals with jurisdiction to apply that law have existed in the decades since the Nuremberg and Tokyo War Crimes Tribunals were dissolved [at the end of World War II].

This situation has changed in the [1990s] with the establishment by the United Nations of the International Tribunal for the Former Yugoslavia and the International Tribunal for Rwanda, with jurisdiction over crimes against humanity, genocide and war crimes committed in those territories. The United Nations is now also in the process of establishing a permanent international criminal court. Moreover, some international investigatory bodies, such as the United Nations Truth Commission for El Salvador, while not international tribunals with criminal jurisdiction, are being created in large measure to pierce national veils of impunity and to fix individual responsibility. The international community is also beginning to develop legal doctrines which would bar governments from granting amnesties to gross violators of human rights, a practice that has tended to be imposed on weak governments by military regimes or other powerful groups before turning over power to civilian authorities.

Expanding Definitions

These responses to new international realities, while still in a formative stage, suggest that the concept of international responsibility for massive violations of human rights is expanding to include individuals and groups in addition to governments. If individuals are deemed to have ever greater rights under the international law of human rights, it makes sense to impose corresponding duties on them not to violate those rights and to hold them internationally responsible for the violation of internationally protected human rights. This approach may in the long run serve as a greater deterrent against human rights violations than the imposition of economic sanctions against a state whose government may either have been powerless at a given time to prevent the violations or have come into power subsequent to their commission.

The international law concepts of state continuity and state responsibility while valid principles, can in today's world have unjust consequences. They may force newly elected governments of impoverished countries to pay compensation for human rights violations committed by their repressive predecessors, without giving them the international support, tools and remedies to make it possible for the responsible individuals to be held internationally liable for their misdeeds. In the absence of such remedies, a newly established democratic government, with economic resources seriously depleted by an oppressive regime, may be made to pay compensation for the human rights violations committed by that regime while its former leaders—those responsible for the violations—live in luxury, frequently abroad, and thus go unpunished. An effective international system to hold these individuals personally liable as a matter of international law and bar domestic amnesties granted under duress would go a long way to deter human rights violations and to ensure a more just approach to this entire problem. The fact that the international community is today moving in this direction is a welcome development.

Protecting Minority Rights

In recent years we have also seen a renewed interest by the international community in the establishment of international norms and institutions for the protection of the rights of individuals belonging to national, racial, ethnic, linguistic or religious minorities. Here it is worth recalling that the United Nations Charter contains a broad non-discrimination clause but makes no reference to minority rights as such. The same is true of the Universal Declaration of Human Rights, which does, however, contain an equal protection clause as well as a non-discrimination provision which is more extensive in scope than that of the Charter. The [U.N.] International Covenant on Civil and Political Rights, adopted in 1966, contains one rather general provision on the subject. It is true, of course, that, to the extent that the [U.N.] Genocide Convention criminalizes acts designed to eradicate national, ethnic, racial or religious groups as such, it can be characterized as an instrument for the protection of the rights of minorities, albeit one which is very limited in scope. On the whole, however, there was relatively little interest in the international community during the formative years of the United Nations and other post-Second World War international and regional organizations in the establishment of international systems for the protection of the rights of minorities. The absence of an appropriate clause on this subject in the United Nations Charter can be attributed, in part at least, to the opposition of some Eastern and Central European nations. These countries believed that various irredentist [separatist] movements in the 1930s, which had been encouraged by [Nazi Germany's leader, Adolf] Hitler and his allies, had their source in the League of Nations [the precursor to the United Nations] minorities system. Whether true or not, the omission of any reference to minorities in the United Nations Charter and the Universal Declaration is related to these sentiments.

The break-up of the Soviet empire [in 1991], the inhuman policies of 'ethnic cleansing' accompanying the dissolution of the former Yugoslavia [began in 1991] and the threats of similar practices in other parts of the world have again focused international attention on the need for the international protection of minorities. Efforts to lay the normative foundation for a system which would accomplish this objective have been initiated in the United Nations with the adoption by the General Assembly of the 1992 Declaration on the Rights of Persons Belonging to National or Ethnic, Religious and Linguistic Minorities; in the Council of Europe [an international organization for security and crisis management established in 1973], with the adoption in 1994 of the Framework Convention for the Protection of National Minorities; and in the framework of the Organization on Security and Co-operation in Europe (OSCE) [an international organization of 46 member States in Europe. They wrote the European Convention on Human Rights in 1950, with the 1990 Copenhagen Concluding Document and a number of later OSCE instruments on the subject, followed in 1992 by the establishment of the Office of the OSCE High Commissioner for National Minorities.

Considering that we live in a world in which extreme nationalism and various forms of racial, ethnic and religious intolerance are on the rise, it is safe to predict that international efforts to protect minorities will increasingly occupy the attention of the international community and result in greater legislative and institutional activities in this area. We may thus be coming full circle from the minorities system established by the League of Nations, its abandonment by the founders of the United Nations, to the realization that current international realities require a revival of the ideas which gave rise to the League system, and the promulgation of a new body of international human rights law on the subject.

Dealing with Large-Scale Human Rights Violations

The United Nations Security Council [the organ of the UN mandated to maintain international peace and security] is today also increasingly taking action to deal with large-scale human rights violations by authorizing enforcement measures under the powers that Chapter VII of the United Nations Charter confers on it. This chapter applies to situations determined by the Security Council to constitute a 'threat to the peace, breach of the peace, or act of aggression'. Such action has been taken by the Security Council in some of its decisions relating to the Kurds in Iraq, to Somalia and to the former Yugoslavia and Haiti, among others. While it is still too early to assert that these and related cases have now firmly established the principle that massive violations of human rights will be deemed by the Security Council to constitute a sufficient legal basis for action under Chapter VII, it is clear that the Security Council is moving in that direction. What we are seeing here is the emergence of a modern version of collective humanitarian intervention which has its basis in the convergence of two important developments: the growing power of the Security Council in the post-Cold War era and the increasing unwillingness of the international community to tolerate massive violations of human rights. Only time will tell whether this ultimate weapon of the international community for dealing with truly egregious violations of human rights will in fact be used to advance the cause of human rights rather than some extraneous political objectives, a practice which brought the old doctrine of humanitarian intervention into bad repute.

Islamic Reactions to Western Ideas of Human Rights

Emile Sahliyeh

In the following article Emile Sahliyeh describes the Islamic reactions to Western human rights standards. Sahliyeh explains that many conservative Islamic groups stand against Western concepts of nation-states, capitalism, and secularism. To these Muslims, social divisions based on nationality, wealth, and race are incompatible with pure Islam. Therefore, human rights that address disparities in these secular realms are unimportant. In effect, according to Sahliyeh, Muslim thinkers believe that the Islamic code of religious law already guarantees rights and freedoms more equitable and just than those of the West. Muslim thinkers have published their own Islamic variation of human rights. Three themes that figure in these writings are the rejection of the universality of human rights, the belief that religion and politics should not be separated, and the duty of individuals to their community and to God. Emile Sahliyeh is associate professor of political science at the University of Northern Texas. Among his publications is the book Religious Resurgence and Politics in the Contemporary World.

The last two decades of the twentieth century witnessed a profusion of articles and books dealing with the status of human rights. The growing attention to human rights is part of larger changes in international relations. These changes include the end of the cold war, the collapse of communism in the Soviet Union and Eastern Europe, the spread of democratization and human rights in different parts of the world, and the globalization of information and market forces. In addition to reporting about the status of human rights, this vast body of literature investigated the conditions that lead governments to repress or respect the rights of their citizens.

The Middle East region has not been excluded from this trend, as the question of human rights has received considerable attention from both the academic community and political activists. In response to a mounting economic crisis and domestic public pressure in the second half of the 1980s, several Middle Eastern countries introduced democratic reforms. This limited democratic reform movement triggered an intense discussion among Middle East-area specialists concerning the prospects for democratization, the barriers to the advancement of human rights, and the persistence of authoritarianism. In the late 1970s and the 1980s a number of human rights groups and movements began to appear in some Middle Eastern countries. It was also during this period that international attention began to focus on the status of human rights in the Middle East. . . .

[The] low record of human rights in the Middle East region has been widely debated in the scholarly literature. The debate is entangled in religious, cultural, and political issues. Some aspects of this literature revolve around the question of whether the Middle East should be judged by the same standards of human rights as the West, or if it should be treated differently when it comes to the question of human rights. . . .

The Islamic Arguments

Since the 1980s an Islamic variant of opposition to Western human rights standards began to dominate the political scene in several Middle Eastern countries. This Islamic alternative took the form of several Islamic opposition movements in countries like Algeria, Tunisia, Egypt, Jordan, Saudi Arabia, Yemen, Afghanistan, Iran, and Sudan. These movements consider Western human rights materialistic, hypocritical, and insincere. Over the centuries the West practiced massive human rights violations—such as racism, religious persecution, slavery, genocide, and exploitation of the Middle East. Like their nationalist counterparts, the Islamic activists consider human rights alien to Islam and a product of Christian culture and Western imperialism and hegemony. They advocate Muslims' struggle against global capitalism, Westernization, and secularism and call for the revitalization of Islamic norms and traditions.

To many of these Islamic groups and conservative thinkers, nationalism, democracy, and human rights and individual freedoms are incompatible with Islamic political norms. The concept of nationalism and the current division of the Islamic world into separate nation-states are inconsistent with the universalism of Islam. Classical Islam believes in the unity of mankind and recognizes only the division of the world into the communities of believers and nonbelievers. Within this community of believers, there is no place for distinction on the bases of color, race, national origin, or language. According to Aziz Ahmed, the Islamic *Umma* "constitutes a harmonious whole in which the claims of the family, community, parents, women, orphans, slaves and unbelievers are duly recognized."

Three Themes of Islamic Human Rights

The United Nations' 1948 endorsement of the Universal Declaration of Human Rights, the 1966 International Covenant on Economic, Social, and Cultural Rights, and the 1966 International Covenant on Civil and Political Rights triggered a debate among these Islamic movements and thinkers concerning the place of human rights in Islam. In reaction to these documents and the increasing saliency of human rights, many of these Muslim thinkers and organizations published several documents articulating an Islamic variation of human rights norms. Among others, these Islamic documents include Sultanhussain Tabandeh's "A Muslim Commentary on the Universal Declaration of Human Rights" Allamah Abu al'Ala Mawdudi's *Human Rights in Islam*, the Muslim Council's "The Universal Islamic Declaration of Human Rights," Al-Azhar's "Draft Islamic Constitution," and the Organization of the Islamic Conference's "The Cairo Declaration of Human Rights."

Several themes figure prominently in the writings of these Islamic thinkers and movements. Thinkers like Mawdudi, Mohammad Aziz Ahmed, Tabandeh, Sayyid Qutb, Ayatollah Ruhollah Khomeini, Al-Ghanoushi, Al-Affendiand, and Al-Turabi invoked cultural relativism to challenge the universal standards of human rights. They rejected the universality of human rights and the dominant position that Western standards preoccupy in the human rights system and condemned those writings that depict Islam as stagnant and inferior. In this connection, Majid Anowar maintains "all major cultures are capable of articulating liberating possibilities without surrendering their memories and faiths."

Another theme in the writings of the conservative thinkers pertains to the relationship between religion and politics. They hold that the separation of religion from politics is the primary cause of all the social and political turmoil and confusion in modern societies. They insist that in their political vision there is no separation between religion and the state. The Islamic *Sharia* [code of religious law] is the supreme ethical value for all Muslims, is the source of all human rights, and is based on divine revelations and not man-made law. The *Sharia* regulates the social, political, and cultural aspects of life and elevates mankind to a higher spiritual level. In this context Al-Turabi contends that an Islamic society governed by *Sharia* values is free from materialism and does not have any conflict between individual rights, freedom, or limits of state authority and obedience to God.

Instead of emphasizing rights, these conservative Islamic thinkers stress the duties of the individual to his or her community, the promotion of its well-being, and the preservation of its unity. In their view rights belong to God and individuals can enjoy these rights when they fulfill their duties toward God. The individual is instructed to develop a "virtuous character" in order to serve as a useful member of the Islamic *Umma*. In this regard Aziz Ahmed maintains: "A true believer is the product of a true environment ... where the individual believer depends upon the Millah [Islamic creed] for the development of his personality as a virtuous character and the Millah acquires a unity of will and purpose through the collective organization of such individual believers."

Islam Doesn't Need Modern Political Institutions

These conservative thinkers are opposed to the adoption of modern standards of human rights and Western democratic political institutions and insist that Islam is a comprehensive, seamless, and absolute religion. In their formulation of the Islamic version of human rights documents, the conservative thinkers premise them on cultural, regional, and religious exclusivity. In this context Mawdudi places the Islamic version of human rights in a much superior position to the modern standards of human rights and laments the Western claim of an exclusive origin for human rights. "Even in this modern age which makes such loud claims of progress and enlightenment, the world has not been able to produce more just and more equitable laws than those given 1400 years ago. It hurts one's feelings that Muslims are in possession of such a splendid and comprehensive system of law and yet they look forward for guidance to those leaders of the West who could not have dreamed of attaining those heights of truth and justice that were achieved a long time ago."

In his book, *Human Rights in Islam*, Mawdudi redefines human rights and gives them an exclusively Islamic framework. He states that Islamic *Sharia* recognized the equality of all human beings and extended to them basic human rights without discrimination on the bases of race, color, language, or national origin. These rights include the right to life, the right to a basic standard of living, the right to property, the emancipation of slaves, the right to justice, and the right to cooperate or not to cooperate. Islam also affirmed the respect for the chastity of all women regardless of their religion. It also accorded religious tolerance to non-Muslim minorities and gave them self-rule and autonomy in managing their local affairs.

The conservative thinkers also state that Islam guarantees freedom of expression for Muslims and non-Muslims alike. In this regard, Section (a) of Article 22 of the Cairo Declaration of Human Rights in Islam stipulates: "Everyone shall have the right to express his opinion freely in such manner as would not be contrary to the principles of the *Sharia*." In addition, the Islamic thinkers affirm that Islam goes beyond guaranteeing these basic freedoms to attend to the welfare of the individual—including food, health, child malnutrition, epidemics, and widespread illiteracy in the Third World. Moreover, Mawdudi points to a set of rules that govern the humane treatment of people during war. These rules differentiate between soldiers and civilians and provide certain protections and guarantees for each. Mawdudi suggests that the Prophet and his immediate successors initiated several rules to guide the behavior of the Muslim fighters during their conquest of the Middle East. These directives include the ban upon killing civilian populations, including women, children, the old, the sick, monks, and people in places of worship. Likewise, these orders provided some protection for the combatants, including the safety of the wounded and the ban on burning the enemy alive, killing prisoners of war, looting, and the destruction of property in the conquered territories. . . .

The Liberal Islamic Response to Human Rights

Whereas conservative Islamic thinkers reject the secular standards of human rights and produce a narrow Islamic version of these rights, liberal Islamic scholars acknowledge the need to reconcile Islamic values with the universal and emancipatory standards of modern human rights. Those writers do not share the belief of their conservative counterparts that Islam and the modern concept of human rights are fundamentally incompatible or that the idea of human rights is simply a tool for spreading Western hegemony and colonialism. While acknowledging the differences between Islamic *Sharia* and modern human rights, the liberal thinkers call for a reinterpretation of the Islamic *Sharia* and its reconciliation with international human rights standards.

In his numerous works, the prominent scholar Abdullahi Ahmed Al-Na'im has taken the lead in scholarly efforts to find ways to reconcile Islam with universal human rights. He introduced an alternative model to the Islamic conservatives' cultural relativist critique of human rights that would account for the viewpoint of the non-Western cultural and religious traditions. His model accepts the standards of the Universal Declaration of Human Rights and its subsequent documents as universally applicable to all human beings regardless of religion, gender, race, or national origin. The model calls for a reconciliation between religion and human rights through the reinterpretation of religion. Three considerations make this reconciliation possible. First, the moral, philosophical, and political bases of the human rights documents are found in different religions. Second, finding a middle ground between religion and human rights is mandated by the contradictions between human rights principles and some religious norms, which resulted from the time lag between the two value systems. Third, reconciliation between religion and human rights is essential for the protection of human rights against abuse by the state.

CHAPTER 2

Worldwide Examples of Human Rights Violations

Uzbekistan's Dictator Is Violating Human Rights

Jonathan Freedland

In the following selection Jonathan Freedland argues that by supporting dictators such as Islam Karimov, the leader of Uzbekistan, the United States is undercutting its doctrine of spreading democracy worldwide. Freedland explains that Karimov has violated human rights during his reign. For example, Karimov's regime has locked up six thousand political prisoners, restricted the practice of religion, and ended freedom of the press. The author describes how Uzbeks' right to protest such violations was trampled on May 13, 2005, when a march was violently suppressed by Karimov's military. Freedland calls on the U.S. government to fully embrace its commitment to democracy and use its political and economic clout to pressure dictatorial regimes to grant greater freedoms to their people. Jonathan Freedland is a columnist at the Manchester Guardian *and the author of* Jacob's Gift: A Journey into the Heart of Belonging.

Think of it as the sonofabitch school of foreign policy. Legend has it that when Franklin D. Roosevelt was confronted with the multiple cruelties of his ally, the Nicaraguan dictator Anastasio Somoza, he replied: "He may be a sonofabitch, but he's our sonofabitch."

More than 60 years on, that serves as a pretty good expression of American, and therefore British, attitudes to Islam Karimov, the tyrant of Tashkent [the capital of Uzbekistan] who has ruled the central Asian republic of Uzbekistan since the break-up of the Soviet Union in 1991.

That he is a sonofabitch is beyond dispute. Like so many despots before him, Karimov has looked to medieval times for

Jonathan Freedland, "Comment and Analysis: He's Our Sonofabitch: The West's Support for the Uzbek Regime Exposes Its Destructive Reliance on Despots and Tyrants," *The Guardian* (UK), May 18, 2005. Copyright 2005 Guardian Newspapers Limited. Reproduced by permission of Guardian News Service, Ltd.

ever more brutal methods of oppression. Hence the return of the cauldron, boiling alive two of his critics in 2002. Uzbekistan holds up to 6,000 political prisoners; independent economic activity has been crushed; religious practice is severely restricted; there is no free press; and the internet is censored. On December 26, when the world was marvelling at Ukraine's orange revolution [a series of protests in 2004 and 2005 in response to allegations of government corruption and electoral fraud], Karimov was hosting an election that was not nearly as close—he had banned all the opposition parties.

Karimov and U.S. Foreign Policy

But, hey, what's a little human rights violation among friends? And Karimov has certainly been our friend. Shortly after [the terrorist attacks of] 9/11, he allowed the U.S. to locate an airbase at Khanabad—a helpful contribution to the upcoming war against Afghanistan [which was invaded on September 18, 2001]. Since then he has been happy to act as a reliable protector of central Asian oil and gas supplies, much coveted by a U.S. eager to reduce its reliance on the [Persian] Gulf states. And he has gladly let Uzbekistan be used for what is euphemistically known as "rendition", the practice of exporting terror suspects to countries less squeamish about torture than Britain or the U.S. This was the matter over which the heroic Craig Murray, the former UK ambassador to Tashkent, fell out with his employers: he argued that Britain was "selling its soul" by using information gathered under such heinous circumstances.

Brushing Murray's qualms to one side, London and Washington remained grateful to Karimov. A procession of top [George W.] Bush administration officials trekked to Tashkent to thank the dictator for his services. [Secretary of Defense] Donald Rumsfeld, not content with that 1983 photo of himself shaking hands with [former Iraq dictator] Saddam Hussein, praised Karimov for his "wonderful cooperation", while

George Bush's former Treasury secretary, Paul O'Neill, admired the autocrat's "very keen intellect and deep passion" for improving the lives of ordinary Uzbeks.

The Uzbek Government's Response to Protesters

And perhaps this egregious example of sonofabitchism would have remained all but unnoticed had it not been for the past few days [before May 18, 2005]. For having ugly friends can only work if people don't look at your companion too closely—and [then] the world saw Karimov in action. When opponents took to the streets [on] Friday [May 13, 2005], the dictator ordered his troops to open fire. Uzbek official figures speak of 169 dead; human rights groups estimate the toll at between 500 and 750—most of them unarmed.

When crowds demonstrated in Lebanon, Ukraine and Georgia, the Americans welcomed it as "people power". But the brave stand in Uzbekistan brought a different response. Washington called for "restraint" from both sides, as if the unarmed civilians were just as guilty as those shooting at them. In the past couple of days, the tune has changed slightly. Now the state department wants Tashkent to "institute real reforms" and address its "human rights problems". It is at least possible that Washington may soon decide Karimov has become an embarrassment and that he should be replaced by a new, friendlier face—but one just as reliable. Less of a sonofabitch, but still ours.

Paying Lip-Service to Democracy

Sonofabitchism has always been an awkward business, even in Roosevelt's day [1933–1945]; it hardly squares with America's image of itself as a beacon in a dark world. But the contradiction—some would call it hypocrisy—is all the greater now. For this is the Bush era, and the Bush doctrine is all about spreading democracy and "the untamed fire of freedom" to the furthest corner of the globe. If that's the rhetoric, then it's hard to reconcile with a reality that involves funneling cash to a man who boils his enemies.

Maybe Bush should just break with the past and fight his war for democracy with pure, democratic means. But that would frighten him. Allow elections in countries now deemed reliable—say Egypt, Saudi Arabia, Jordan, Morocco—and who knows what havoc might be unleashed? Washington fears it would lose its friends, only to see them replaced by the enemy itself: radical Islamists, the force most likely to win democratic contests in large swaths of the Arab world.

That is the conundrum. And yet the case that America, and Britain for that matter, should not only talk the democratic talk but walk the democratic walk is powerful—and not only in pure, idealistic terms. This argument has realpolitik [foreign policy based on practical concerns rather than ideals or ethics] on its side, too.

First, despots make bad allies—who all too often become adversaries. Let us recall two men who once played the role of America's sonofabitch. In the 80s, the U.S. backed Saddam against Iran and Osama bin Laden against the Soviets. The US gave those men the guns that would eventually be turned on itself.

Second, pragmatic pacts with the devil don't work. For one thing, by repressing their peoples, tyrannies foment, not prevent, terrorism. But such deals in the name of democracy also taint the very cause they are meant to serve. Thus liberal reformers across the Middle East now struggle to make their case to Arab publics who have grown suspicious that "democracy" means US occupation, a sell-off of oil and Abu Ghraib [a military prison in Iraq where US military officials tortured prisoners in October 2004].

Third, if democracy really is the panacea the Bush doctrine insists it is, then shouldn't it be trusted to work its magic? Put another way, surely a government that truly represented its people would bring the freedom and stability Washington yearns for—regardless of its political complexion?

Perhaps most reassuring to policymakers would be this fact. Even Middle Eastern democrats themselves are not calling for an overnight revolution; they know that in their stifled societies the only public sphere that exists, besides the state, is the mosque. It is for that reason that if elections were held tomorrow in, say, Egypt, the Muslim Brotherhood would take power.

But if the west made the vast financial and military aid it already gives to these regimes conditional on perhaps a three-year programme of gradual liberalisation—lifting emergency laws, allowing proper funding of political parties—then soon some space would open up, terrain occupied neither by the despots nor the mullahs. Different parties and forces could start organising for a future ballot in which they had a decent shot at success.

That surely would be more logically consistent than the current, contradictory reliance on tyrants to advance the cause of freedom. And it might have a chance of working in practice—even in a place as benighted as Uzbekistan.

China Is Committing Numerous Human Rights Violations

Amnesty International

Amnesty International [AI] is the largest international human rights watchdog organization. It produces yearly reports on the state of human rights in all areas of the globe. In the following 2005 report on China, AI states that despite some progress in human rights reform, the nation is still plagued by human rights abuses. AI maintains that China's political leadership routinely censors media and rounds up social dissidents in order to preserve control of the nation. The government has labeled the Falun Gong spiritual movement as a traitorous organization and imprisoned its practitioners, and the authorities continue to persecute the Islamic Uighur minority as terrorists for their desire to secede from China. Amnesty International also laments the fact that those detained for resisting government tyranny have few legal rights and may be subject to arbitrary torture and imprisonment.

The new administration, which had taken office in March 2003, consolidated its authority, particularly following the resignation of former president Jiang Zemin as chair of the Central Military Commission in September. Some legal reforms were introduced, including new regulations aimed at preventing torture in police custody and an amendment to the Constitution in March stating that "the state respects and protects human rights." However, the failure to introduce necessary institutional reforms severely compromised the enforcement of these measures in practice.

The authorities took a more proactive approach towards dealing with China's HIV/AIDS epidemic, including a new law

Amnesty International, "Amnesty International, Report 2005: China," 2005. Reproduced by permission.

in August aimed at strengthening AIDS prevention and stopping discrimination against those living with AIDS or other infectious diseases. However, grassroots activists campaigning for better treatment continued to be arbitrarily detained.

Political crackdowns continued on specific groups, including the Falun Gong spiritual movement, unofficial Christian groups, and so-called "separatists" and "religious extremists" in Xinjiang and Tibet....

Persecuting Human Rights Defenders

The authorities continued to use provisions of the Criminal Law relating to "subversion", "state secrets" and other vaguely defined national security offences to prosecute peaceful activists and advocates of reform. Lawyers, journalists, HIV/AIDS activists and housing rights advocates were among those harassed, detained or imprisoned for documenting human rights abuses, campaigning for reform, or attempting to obtain redress for victims of violations.

- Ding Zilin, who set up the "Tiananmen Mothers" group to campaign for justice following the killing of her son in Beijing on 4 June 1989, was detained by the police in March [2004] to prevent her from highlighting her concerns. She was also placed under a form of house arrest a few days before the 15th anniversary of the crackdown to prevent her from filing a legal complaint on behalf of 126 others who also lost relatives in 1989.

- Li Dan, an AIDS activist, was detained by police in Henan province in August [2004] in an apparent attempt to prevent him from protesting against the government's handling of the AIDS epidemic. He was released one day later but then beaten up by two unknown assailants. Li Dan had founded a school for AIDS orphans in the province where up to one million people are believed to have become HIV-positive after selling their blood plasma to unsanitary, state-sanctioned blood collection stations. The school had been closed down by the local authorities in July [2004].

Violations in the Context of Economic Reform

The rights of freedom of expression and association of workers' representatives continued to be severely curtailed and independent trade unions remained illegal. In the context of economic restructuring, large numbers of people were reportedly denied adequate reparations for forcible eviction, land requisition and job layoffs. Public and largely peaceful protests against such practices increased, leading to numerous detentions and other abuses.

Beijing was often the focus for such protests due in part to house demolitions during the city's preparations for the Olympics in 2008. People also travelled to Beijing from other parts of the country to petition the central authorities after failing to obtain redress at the local level. Tens of thousands of petitioners were reportedly detained by Beijing police during security operations in advance of official meetings in March and September [2005]. . . .

Violence Against Women

Numerous articles about domestic violence appeared in the national media, reflecting widespread concern that such abuses were not being effectively addressed.

Serious violations against women and girls continued to be reported as a result of the enforcement of the family planning policy, including forced abortions and sterilizations. In July [2004] the authorities publicly reinforced a ban on the selective abortion of female foetuses in an attempt to reverse a growing gap in the boy-girl birth ratio.

Women in detention, including large numbers of Falun Gong practitioners, remained at risk of torture, including rape and sexual abuse. . . .

Political Activists and Internet Users

Political activists, including supporters of banned political groups, or those calling for political change or greater democracy continued to be arbitrarily detained and in some cases sentenced and imprisoned. By the end of [2005], AI had records of more than 50 people who had been detained or imprisoned after accessing or circulating politically sensitive information on the Internet.

- Kong Youping, a leading member of the Chinese Democratic Party and former union activist in Liaoning province, was sentenced to 15 years' imprisonment in September for "subversion". He had been detained in late 2003 after posting articles on the Internet attacking official corruption and urging a reassessment of the 1989 pro-democracy movement.

Repression of Spiritual and Religious Groups

The Falun Gong spiritual movement remained a key target of repression, which reportedly included many arbitrary detentions. Most of those detained were assigned to periods of "Re-education through Labour" without charge or trial, during which they were at high risk of torture or ill-treatment, particularly if they refused to renounce their beliefs. Others were held in prisons and psychiatric hospitals. According to overseas Falun Gong sources, more than 1,000 people detained in connection with the Falun Gong had died since the organization was banned in 1999, mostly as a result of torture or ill-treatment.

Other so-called "heretical organizations" and unofficial religious groups were also targeted. Reports increased of arrests and detentions of unregistered Catholics and members of unofficial Protestant "house churches". Those attempting to document such violations and send reports overseas were also at risk of arrest.

- Zhang Shengqi, Xu Yonghai and Liu Fenggang, three independent Protestant activists, were sentenced to one, two and three years in prison respectively by the Hangzhou Intermediate People's Court for "leaking state secrets" in August. The charges related to passing information abroad about crackdowns on Protestants and the closure of unofficial churches in the area.

Death Penalty and Torture

The death penalty continued to be used extensively and arbitrarily, at times as a result of political interference. People were executed for non-violent crimes such as tax fraud and embezzlement as well as drug offences and violent crimes. The authorities continued to keep national statistics on death sentences and executions secret. Based on public reports available, AI estimated that at least 3,400 people had been executed and at least 6,000 sentenced to death by the end of the year, although the true figures were believed to be much higher. In March, a senior member of the National People's Congress announced that China executes around 10,000 people per year.

A lack of basic safeguards protecting the rights of defendants meant that large numbers of people continued to be sentenced to death and executed after unfair trials. In October [2004], the authorities announced an intention to reinstate Supreme Court review of death penalty cases and to introduce other legal reforms aimed at safeguarding the rights of criminal suspects and defendants. It remained unclear, however, when these measures would be introduced. . . .

Torture and ill-treatment continued to be reported in a wide variety of state institutions despite the introduction of several new regulations aimed at curbing the practice. Common methods included kicking, beating, electric shocks, suspension by the arms, shackling in painful positions, and sleep and food deprivation. Political interference in the rule of law, restricted access to the outside world for detainees, and a failure to establish effective mechanisms for complaint and investigation continued to be key factors allowing the practice to flourish.

The authorities officially announced an intention to reform "Re-education through Labour", a system of administrative detention used to detain hundreds of thousands of people for up to four years without charge or trial. However, the exact nature and scope of reform remained unclear.

People accused of political or criminal offences continued to be denied due process. Detainees' access to lawyers and family members continued to be severely restricted and trials fell far short of international fair trial standards. . . .

Xinjiang Uighur Autonomous Region

The authorities continued to use the "global war on terror" to justify harsh repression in Xinjiang, resulting in serious human rights violations against the ethnic Uighur community [a Turkic people who want to reestablish the state of East Turkistan in the Xinjiang region]. The authorities continued to make little distinction between acts of violence and acts of passive resistance. Repression resulted in the closure of unofficial mosques, arrests of imams, restrictions on the use of the Uighur language and the banning of certain Uighur books and journals.

Arrests of so-called "separatists, terrorists and religious extremists" continued and thousands of political prisoners, including prisoners of conscience, remained in prison. Many of those charged with "separatist" or "terrorist" offences were reportedly sentenced to death and executed. Uighur activists attempting to pass information abroad about the extent of the crackdown were at risk of arbitrary detention and imprisonment.

China continued to use "counter-terrorism" as a means to strengthen its political and economic ties with neighbouring states. Uighurs who had fled to Central Asia, Pakistan, Nepal and other states, including asylum-seekers and refugees, remained at serious risk of forcible return to China. China continued to put pressure on the USA to return 22 Uighurs held in the US detention camp in Guantánamo Bay, Cuba. In June, the US authorities stated that the Uighurs would not be returned to China due to fears that they would be tortured or executed.

Ethnic Conflict in Sudan Is Causing Large-Scale Human Rights Violations

Nsongurua J. Udombana

In the following selection, author Nsongurua J. Udombana explains that the ethnic conflict in Sudan, a country in northeastern Africa, presents a challenge to the United Nations and the African Union. He says that the government of Sudan and government-backed militias have committed large-scale human rights violations that warrant humanitarian military intervention. Since 1956 Arab-dominated northern Sudan and predominantly black Christian and animist southern Sudan have been fighting a civil war over land and resources. The Arab-controlled government of Sudan has favored the Arab claims, and in 1986 the government began arming Arab militias and using them to fight rebels in southern Sudan. Udombana explains that the current crisis began in 2003 when rebel forces, claiming years of abuse and neglect by the Arab-dominated government, attacked government military forces in the western province of Darfur. In response, a government-supported militia initiated a campaign of ethnic cleansing in which all black citizens of Darfur have been targeted. Udombana writes that the militia robbed, raped, forcibly displaced, or killed untold numbers of innocent civilians in Darfur. Many villages have been destroyed, and as of November 2005 the death toll was estimated to be between 300,000 and 340,000. Udombana argues that the United Nations and the African Union should not allow the Sudanese government to continue its murderous campaign.

Nsongurua Udombana is an associate professor and director of the Human Rights Center at Central European University in

Budapest. Udombana has also worked as a research fellow at the Danish Center for Human Rights.

Since early 2003, the world has watched with both shock and apathy as Sudan's Arab-dominated government ethnically cleanses its vast western region of Darfur by arming, encouraging, and giving air support to mostly Arab militias who kill, maim, rape, and rob black Africans. The Darfur crisis combines the worst of everything: armed conflict, extreme violence, sexual assault, great tides of desperate refugees— without even the unleavened bread of a desperate escape, hunger, and disease, all uniting with an unforgiving desert climate. Evidence from numerous sources—governmental, intergovernmental, and nongovernmental—suggests a tragedy that, in nature and scale, follows in the example of the Holocaust. Such atrocious, terrorizing, and hideous acts, coupled with impunity by the Government of Sudan (GoS), present grave challenges to contemporary international law and institutions that the international community has painstakingly fashioned out to preserve modern civilization.

The Challenges of Darfur

From a global perspective, Darfur is a challenge to the United Nations' (UN) norms on peace, security, human rights, and refugee issues. The UN itself was established, inter alia [among other things], "[t]o maintain international peace and security, and to that end: to take effective collective measures for the prevention and removal of threats to the peace" and to achieve "international co-operation in solving international problems of [a] . . . humanitarian character." Darfur is a challenge, more particularly, to the United Nations Security Council (UNSC) [one of 6 organs of the UN], which is mandated to maintain international peace and security and, to this effect, to determine the existence of any threat to, or breach of, the peace and to make recommendations or decide what measures are to be taken to maintain or restore international peace and security. Darfur is a challenge to many UN agencies, including the High Commissioner for Human Rights (UNHCHR), established in 1993 to promote and protect human rights throughout the world. Given the humanitarian issues in Darfur, including the mass exodus of refugees to neighboring states, Darfur is also a challenge to the High Commissioner for Refugees (UNHCR) and the International Committee of the Red Cross (ICRC).

From a regional perspective, Darfur is a challenge to the African Union (AU), established by its Constitutive Act of 2000 inter alia "to take up the multifaceted challenges that confront" Africa and its peoples including the promotion of peace, security, and stability in the continent. It is a challenge especially to the Peace and Security Council (PSC), which is not merely an organ of the AU but is, more significantly, the "standing decision-making organ for the prevention, management and resolution of conflicts." Of course, Darfur is a challenge to the human rights community in Africa, especially the African Commission on Human and Peoples' Rights (African Commission), established in 1987 to promote and protect human and peoples' rights and ensure their protection in Africa.

The Darfur crisis brings to the fore the debate on the "right" to humanitarian military intervention (HMI) in international law, a debate that this article seeks to reexamine. Do the abuses in Darfur meet any standard required for the use of military force in Sudan; or will such an action amount to a violation of Sudan's territorial sovereignty, especially as the GoS claims the Darfur crisis is its internal affair? This article argues that, in the context of a military counterinsurgency campaign against rebel groups, the GoS and government-backed ethnic militias have committed grave international crimes—genocide, "ethnic cleansing," war crimes, and crimes against humanity—in Darfur to justify HMI, particularly because diplomacy has failed to jolt the GoS into halting the mayhem. This article denounces the current posture of neutrality that the international community is taking in Sudan, despite the overwhelming evidence of continuing atrocities and gross violations of human rights in Darfur. Such neutrality helps the killers and not the victims. . . .

The Land, People and Crisis of Darfur

Sudan is the largest country in Africa, slightly more than one-quarter the size of the United States (US). The Nile and its tributaries dominate Sudan, which has a territory spanning about 2.5 million square kilometers and a population of about 40 million. Sudan borders Egypt in the North; the Red Sea, Eritrea, and Ethiopia in the East; Uganda, Kenya, and the misleadingly renamed Democratic Republic (DR) of the Congo in the South; and the Central African Republic (CAR), Chad, and Libya in the West. Sudan is rich in minerals, including petroleum, small reserves of iron ore, copper, chromium ore, zinc, tungsten, mica, silver, gold, and hydropower. Since it gained independence from the United Kingdom (UK) in 1956, however, the country has been embroiled in a civil war between the Arab-dominated North and the Christian and animist [nature worshipping] South—a war that is rooted in economic, political, and social factors. The Sudanese conflict is the longest in Africa, with serious human rights abuses and humanitarian disasters.

Darfur is Sudan's largest region, situated on its western border with Libya, Chad, and the CAR. It comprises an area of approximately 250,000 square kilometers—"an enormous region about the size of France"—with an estimated population of 6 million persons. 15 Sedentary African farmers, such as the Fur, Masalit, and Zaghawa tribes, predominate Darfur, with the Fur and Masalit as dominant ethnic groups. These dominant tribes have often united in marriage with Arabs and other Africans. The rest of the population of Darfur consists of nomadic Arab tribes. Although both the black African and the Arab tribes are Muslims, they have a long-standing history of clashes over land, crops, and resources.

For years, the central government in Khartoum has favored the Arabs in Darfur, leading to distrust by the Fur leaders. The distrust became exacerbated when the Sadiq El Mahdi government (1986–1989) adopted a policy of arming Arab Baggara militias from Darfur and Kordofan known as "muraheleen" and using them as a counterinsurgency force against the southern-based rebels. Both the El Mahdi government and its military successors have employed these militias for almost twenty years. After taking power in a coup in 1989, the National Islamic Front (NIF), renamed the National Congress, incorporated many of the muraheleen into the Popular Defense Forces and paramilitaries, who have been involved in attacks against the Fur community in Darfur, raiding, looting, displacing, enslaving, and punishing the Dinka and Nuer civilians.

The present crisis in Darfur commenced in February 2003, largely as a result of actions by rebel forces, notably the Sudanese Liberation Army (SLA), and later the Justice and Equality Movement (JEM), the members of whom come primarily from the Zaghawa, Fur, and Masalit tribes. The SLA and the JEM accused the Arab-ruled GoS of decades of malign, neglect, and oppression of black Africans in favor of Arabs, necessitating their resort to violence to shake off a yoke they would rather not shoulder. They also demanded that the GoS address perceived political marginalization, socioeconomic neglect, and discrimination towards African Darfurians by successive federal governments in Khartoum. These are common themes in Africa, largely because the post-colonial state structures "tend toward the institutionalization of ethnic entitlements, rights, and privileges, which create differentiated and unequal status of citizenship." A group consigned to a permanent minority status will never consider the political arrangement as just.

On 24 and 25 April 2003, the SLA attacked government military forces at El Fasher in north Darfur. Because the GoS apparently was not in possession of sufficient military resources, as many of its forces were still located in the south, it allegedly sponsored a militia, composed of a loose collection of fighters mostly of Arab background, known as the "Janjaweed," to respond to the rebellion. With active government support, the militias attacked villages, systematically targeting civilian communities that share the same ethnicity as the rebel groups, killing, looting, forcibly displacing, destroying hundreds of villages, and polluting water supplies. There have been reports of deliberate aggressions against women and girls, including gang rapes, during the invasions, with women and girls abducted, held in confinement for several days, and repeatedly raped. Other forms of sexual violence have been reported, especially during flight and further displacement, including when women have left towns and IDP [internally displaced persons] sites to collect wood or water. Some women and girls have become pregnant as a result of rape, and some have been charged with Zina—unlawful sexual intercourse, which is a punishable offense under the Sudan Penal Code—for acts in which they did not willingly engage! Many children—boys and girls—have been abducted, killed, and generally made to suffer the devastating consequences of the problems caused by adults, acts that clearly violate both customary and conventional law prohibitions of deliberate attacks on civilians. More than one million villagers have been forced from their homes, fleeing to refugee camps in Sudan and Eastern Chad.

It is hard to know the total mortality during the two years of ethnic cleansing in Darfur, partly because the GoS initially blocked the teams from the UN and other agencies from going there to make such an estimate. The Darfur Commission Report also failed to give any kind of death toll from the crisis, despite cataloging hundreds of violent incidents and many eyewitness accounts of village massacres. It only established "two irrefutable facts regarding the situation in Darfur: first, that 1.65 million persons have been internally displaced in Darfur, with more than 200,000 refugees in neighboring Chad; and, second, that there has been large-scale destruction of villages throughout the three states of Darfur. The current estimates of the number of deaths range between 300,000 and 340,000. A British parliamentary report, released in 2005, also put the total death toll at 300,000," while Jan Egeland, the UN emergency relief coordinator, put the number of those who have died from hunger and disease at 180,000. The death toll is rising by about 10,000 per month.

The cycle of violence in Darfur has continued unabated, even in villages in which there is nothing left to burn and loot; and the fear that it will continue has paralyzed refugees and displaced populations, preventing voluntary returns, trapping them in camps or informal settlements for the foreseeable future. One possible explanation for the very cruel and disproportionate response to the uprising in Darfur may be that the GoS was not in the mood to tolerate further threats to its authority. Thus, as the Commission on Human Rights (CHR) puts it, "what appears to have been an ethnically based rebellion has been met with an ethnically based response, building in large part on long-standing, but largely hitherto contained, tribal rivalries." The humanitarian consequences of the conflict have been aggravated particularly by the refusal of the GoS to allow unrestricted access to Darfur by humanitarian agencies. In 2004, the US Agency for International Development reported: "Humanitarian access to conflict affected populations outside of the state capitals of Geneina, El Fasher, and Nyala was extremely limited until late May due to GoS impediments that blocked humanitarian access and relief operations." The GoS, of course, has denied the charges and even described the Janjaweed militias as "criminals," though the police have yet to investigate, let alone prosecute, the bandits.

There are even "widespread and confirmed allegations that some members of the Janjaweed have been incorporated into the police." President El-Bashir himself also reportedly confirmed to the media that, in order to rein in the Janjaweed, these same militias "were incorporated in other areas such as the armed forces and the police."

Surely, the testimonies of survivors, international aid workers, foreign observers, and even militia leaders themselves all flatly contradict the lies from Khartoum. The UN Special Rapporteur on Extrajudicial, Arbitrary or Summary Executions indicated on 29 June 2003 that significant evidence exists to support allegations that the GoS helped perpetuate grave human rights violations in Darfur, stating that it was the GoS' responsibility to end the cycle of violence and the culture of impunity. Human Rights Watch has also shown evidence that the Sudanese military is supporting and aiding the Janjaweed attacks and permitting the militias to maintain at least sixteen camps in the western region of Darfur. The Darfur Commission Report removes any iota of doubt regarding the involvement of the GoS in the mayhem. The report established clear links between the GoS and the Janjaweed militias and stated that militias "have received weapons, and regular supplies of ammunition which have been distributed to the militias by the army, by senior civilian authorities at the locality level."

The United States Is Violating the Human Rights of Suspected Terrorist Prisoners

Michael Ratner

In the following excerpt Michael Ratner describes the predicament of prisoners at the United States prison camp in Guantánamo Bay, Cuba. He explains that many of the prisoners there were captured or arrested during U.S. military operations in Afghanistan since the terrorist attacks of September 11, 2001, and the subsequent invasion of Afghanistan in October. These prisoners are being held because of their alleged ties to terrorism. Ratner argues that articles 9, 10, and 11 of the Universal Declaration of Human Rights guarantee all people freedom from arbitrary arrest, the right to a fair public hearing, and the right to be presumed innocent until proven guilty. However, according to Ratner, many of the prisoners at Guantánamo Bay have been denied the basic human right of a court hearing. They have been held without being formally accused of a crime and they have been interrogated, coerced, and denied access to legal counsel. Ratner uses these and several other examples to illustrate the magnitude of the human rights violations that the United States is committing at the Guantánamo Bay prison camp.

Michael Ratner is currently serving as attorney and vice president at the Center for Constitutional Rights. He is also a Skelly Wright Fellow at Yale Law School and a lecturer at Columbia Law School. He has written and cowritten numerous books on international law, including in 1996 International Human Rights: Litigation in U.S. Courts.

Michael Ratner, "The Guantánamo Prisoners," in *America's Disappeared: Detainees, Secret Imprisonment, and the War on Terror.* New York: Seven Stories Press, 2005.

It has been called an "American Gulag," "A Lawless Human Warehouse," "A Legal Black Hole," "A Glimpse into Our Future," "A Cold Storage Facility," and the "First Off shore Concentration Camp of the Empire." The entire world knows it by these epithets: it is the United States prison camp at Guantánamo Bay, Cuba.

It is a prison—or rather a number of prisons—that as of this writing [2005] hold approximately 550 human beings from over 40 countries. Most of the detainees were captured, kidnapped, or arrested—oftentimes on the basis of unreliable information—during the U.S. military operations that have been occurring in Afghanistan since 9/11. Most of the detainees have been held incommunicado for more than two years. We do not know most of their names, as the United States will not give out this information. To date, only four have been charged with crimes. Each detainee may have been interrogated as many as 200 times. Almost none have had access to an attorney, or have had contact with their families. None have had access to any court or judicial process for asserting their innocence. They could be held forever. These are executive detentions totally outside both domestic and international law. The detainees are truly America's disappeared. . . .

What Is Known About the Detainees

Not much is known about those imprisoned in Guantánamo; certainly, nothing is known publicly as to what crimes—if any—individual detainees are suspected of having committed. Because so little is known, it is impossible to verify the government's claims regarding their dangerousness or commitment to terrorism, or to know if any are there by mistake. Few attorneys, and no family or press are allowed to speak with the detainees, but the International Committee of the Red Cross has a regular presence in Guantánamo and presumably has visited the prison and the detainees. Allegedly the Red Cross has written a number of reports to U.S. officials criticizing the conditions at Guantánamo and the interrogation techniques used there. However, those reports have not been made public, and as is standard with the Red Cross, it has said nothing regarding the condition of individual detainees.

The U.S. administration has made public statements regarding the alleged character of those detained, without allowing any of the detainees access to attorneys to help them refute these claims. At the time of the transfers to Guantánamo, Secretary of Defense Donald Rumsfeld called the detainees "hardened criminals willing to kill themselves and others for their cause." Emphasizing their dangerousness, he said, "Every time people have messed with these folks, they've gotten in trouble. And they are very well trained. They're willing to give up their lives, in many instances." The U.S. military officials in charge of the prison said they were told to expect "the worst of the worst." "These are the worst of a very bad lot," said Vice President Cheney. "They are very dangerous."

The Tribunals Do Not Satisfy Requirements

There may well be terrorists among those imprisoned. However, until the Supreme Court forced it to do so in June 2004, the United States failed to bring anyone before any kind of tribunal or court to determine who is a terrorist, who is a prisoner of war, and who is an innocent civilian. On July 30, 2004, the first tribunals opened for business, and on August 13, 2004, they issued their first rulings. "Lawyers for some of the detainees," reported the *New York Times* following the first rulings, "said the tribunals, known formally as Combatant Status Review Tribunals, did not comply with the rulings of the Supreme Court in June requiring that people held as unlawful enemy combatants be able to challenge their detentions in a fair proceeding with due process protections. . . . Lawyers for the detainees say federal court is the proper forum for adjudicating their rights."

Critics of the Guantánamo tribunals say they do not satisfy the Supreme Court's requirements. Detainees, according to the July order establishing the tribunals, are provided with military officers, not lawyers, to act as their "personal representatives"; the representatives may review only "reasonably available information"; the detainee may call only "reasonably available witnesses"; the tribunals are made up of "three neutral commissioned officers of the U.S. Armed Forces," not independent judges, and the rules of evidence do not apply.

The detainees who went through the first four tribunals were held to be properly designated as "enemy combatants" and according to these tribunals may be held indefinitely.

Despite these rulings however, and based on information from the hundreds of persons who have been released so far, it appears that the United States is exaggerating by portraying many of those at Guantánamo as terrorists. These releases, sometimes after over two years in Guantánamo, demonstrate that the administration's sweeping rhetoric has been overblown. If these men are some of the "worst of the worst," how come many were never charged with any crime, by any country? And why did it take so long to determine that they were not terrorists?

Abassin Sayed's Story

In May 2003, after over a year at Guantánamo, the [George W.] Bush administration freed prisoner number 671, Abassin Sayed. After his release, a reporter found him in Afghanistan driving his taxi and playing Hindi music on his radio. Sayed's story reveals a lot about those still imprisoned at Guantánamo.

In April 2002 Sayed was driving his taxi when a gang of local Afghans stopped him at a checkpoint. American soldiers were being ambushed in the area and wanted to capture those responsible. The local Afghans were only too glad to help out, even if those stopped were not involved in the attacks. Although he protested that he was only a taxi driver, Abassin Sayed was turned over to the Americans.

Abassin Sayed never had a chance to prove that he was innocent and was never given any legal process. He was taken to the U.S. airbase at Bagram, Afghanistan, spent a month in an Afghan jail, and then was flown to Guantánamo, where he arrived tied, gagged, masked, and outfitted with dark goggles. He said of his arrival, "It was the act of an animal to treat a human being like that. It was the worst day of my life." He was put into a small cell with the lights on 24 hours a day. As he said, "The lights were so strong, you couldn't differentiate between day and night. If you tried to cover your face to sleep, the soldiers came in and told you not to do that."

When Sayed was found exercising in his cell, he was punished with five days of solitary confinement and was denied blankets and other basic amenities. He was interrogated eleven times for six or seven hours at a time. He was punished in a similar fashion for being unable to answer questions during interrogation. And yet, Sayed's treatment was by no means the most severe; other prisoners are reported to have been interrogated over one hundred times.

Abassin Sayed's best friend, also a taxi driver, is still detained in Guantánamo. His crime? He had asked what had happened to his friend Abassin Sayed after he had been arrested; just for asking, he too was arrested, turned over to the United States, and shipped off to Guantánamo.

Guantánamo Holds Many Innocent Victims

Abassin Sayed's case is not unique. The U.S. military dropped leaflets in Afghanistan offering large sums of money for information leading to the capture of terrorists. Many apparently took up the offer and turned in innocent civilians for their bounty. A military interrogator at Camp Delta estimates that as many as 20 percent of the men in captivity at Guantánamo are innocent. Dozens of prisoners—if not more—are described in U.S. intelligence reports as farmers, taxi drivers, laborers, and shoemakers. According to these reports, at least 59 individuals from Afghanistan and Pakistan were captured and shipped off to Guantánamo despite not fitting the screening criteria for such a transfer. As one military official who served as an interrogator observed, "If they weren't terrorists before, they certainly could be now."

In October 2002 three Afghani men were released after spending almost one year in captivity at Guantánamo. One of the released men reported that he was 105 years old. *New York Times* reporter David Rhode described him in the following manner: "Babbling at times like a child, the partially deaf, shriveled old man was unable to answer the simplest questions." When asked if he was angry with American soldiers, he said that he did not mind, because they "took my old clothes and gave me new clothes." A second Afghani man, released at the same time, said that he was 90 years old and was described as a "wizened old man with a cane" who had been arrested in a raid on his village.

A third, younger man said that he had been cut off from the outside world for eleven months and had only received a letter from his family three days before he was to leave Guantánamo. He said that he was confined to his cell 24 hours a day with only two 15-minute breaks for exercise a week. This third man admitted that he had fought with the Taliban, but said that he had been forced to do so. After he surrendered, he said, soldiers of the warlord Abdul Rashid Dostum falsely told the United States that he and nine others were Taliban officials. His release appears to confirm the essential elements of his story. These men are hardly the "worst of the worst." Here were men who should have never been taken to Guantánamo. Here were men who, had there been a fair hearing before some form of a tribunal, would have been freed long ago.

Coercion Leads to False Testimony

Two other men were freed from Guantánamo in early 2004—
Asif Iqbal and Shafiq Rasul. They were from Tipton, England,
and had initially traveled to Pakistan prior to 9/11 for the
purpose of a marriage arranged by Iqbal's parents. This author met with them in England shortly after their release and
was stunned by their story. They are presently 22 years old,
which means they were picked up when they were 20. At the
time of the meeting they were quite open about discussing the
horrors they had undergone. They had been captured by a
warlord of the Northern Alliance [U.S. allies in Afghanistan]
and had almost died when they were imprisoned in sweltering
shipping containers in Afghanistan (fewer than 30 of the 300
imprisoned in the container survived) before being turned
over to the Americans, presumably for money. In Afghanistan
they were treated brutally by American forces and eventually
shipped off to Guantánamo. They describe the abuse and torture they suffered there . . . in a 115-page personal report
available on the Center for Constitutional Right's web site.

Iqbal and Rasul's case illustrates not only the brutality of
Guantánamo but also the unreliable nature of information
gained by coercive interrogation techniques. U.S. interrogation
officers showed the two a video of Osama bin Laden [the
leader of the al-Qaeda terrorist organization] and claimed that
two of the young men in the video were Iqbal and Rasul.
They denied it, indicated that they were in the UK at the time
and offered to prove it, and pointed out that the men did not
look like them. The interrogator refused to believe them, used
coercive measures, and after three months the young men
"confessed" that it was them in the video.

By this time a real movement against the Guantánamo detentions began emerging in the UK. Eventually British intelligence, MI5, proved to the United States that Iqbal and Rasul
were in the UK at the time the video was made, and that it
could not have been them in the video. There are a lot of les-

sons here: One of the most important is that coercion begets false confessions and destroys people's lives. Another is that Iqbal and Rasul should never have been sent to Guantánamo—a hearing might have resolved their case a lot earlier.

More Information Is Emerging About Detainees

Information about other detainees is also available through their families, as well as from delegations of foreign officials who have been permitted to visit. Some prisoners have been able to send short, censored letters to their families through the Red Cross. These letters are few and far between. A few families that have received letters have contacted lawyers and have asked them to file lawsuits on their sons' behalf. As a result, further information has emerged about the detainees.

For example, according to his family, Australian citizen Mamdouh Habib traveled to Pakistan in August 2001 to look for work and for a school for his two teenage sons. On October 5, 2002—just before he was about to return to Australia and two days before the United States attacked Afghanistan—he was detained by Pakistani officials. He was transported to Egypt, held there for a period of time, apparently tortured, and eventually turned over to the United States and imprisoned at Guantánamo. Obviously, he was nowhere near the fighting in Afghanistan.

Similarly, a delegation from Pakistan that visited Guantánamo concluded that almost all of the 58 Pakistanis detained were low-level foot soldiers and had no link to al Qaeda. Some of these men may have been imprisoned because of the bounty offered for capturing members of al Qaeda and the Taliban. After the delegation's visit, Pakistan requested the release of nearly all of the Pakistani prisoners. The request was granted in September 2004.

Amazingly, it is not only adults who are imprisoned in Guantánamo. Children are there as well. The current number is unknown, but in early 2004 three minors between 13 and 15 years old were freed. The International Committee of the Red Cross issued a statement shortly thereafter stating that Guantánamo was an inappropriate place to detain juveniles and that their detention posed a grave risk to their well-being. Detentions of juveniles at Guantánamo also violates the Optional Protocol to the Convention on the Rights of Children, which requires governments to rehabilitate former children soldiers (assuming this is what the captured children are). As Human Rights Watch has said, "Rehabilitation does not happen at Guantánamo." International law establishes the right of families to maintain contact with their children, the right to a speedy determination of their children's cases, and that detention only be used as a last resort. It appears that the United States has violated—and is violating—each of these rights and requirements. In response to pressure from human rights groups, the United States now imprisons most children at a separate detention facility called Camp Iguana, but children 16 years and older continue to be held captive with the adult detainees at Camp Delta.

These stories of the innocent, of detainees not involved in any fighting, of detainees who were no more than foot soldiers, and of young children, demonstrate the importance of a legal process for determining the status of those imprisoned at Guantánamo, and of the callousness and inhumanity with which the United States is running its lawless prison camp.

CHAPTER 3

How Can Human Rights Be Protected or Improved?

Democracy Promotes Human Rights

G. Shabbir Cheema

In the following excerpt from his book Building Democratic Institutions: Governance Reform in Developing Countries, *G. Shabbir Cheema argues that democracy and human rights are fundamentally linked. He explains that effective democracy depends on human rights and that it is impossible to promote human rights in a country where there is no democracy. Cheema states that the essential characteristics of democracy are even based on human rights. These characteristics are fair elections, independent media, government accountability, a multiparty system, and multiple levels of government. Cheema says that these elements of democracy are intended to protect the rights and basic freedoms of all citizens. Therefore, Cheema emphasizes that, to avoid the marginalization of minorities, a democratic system must include protection for minority rights and a means for minorities to share in economic and political power. G. Shabbir Cheema is the principal adviser on governance in the development and governance division of the Bureau for Development Policy at the United Nations Development Programme. In the past he has taught at the University of Hawaii and New York University.*

Historically, human rights and democracy have been treated as distinct phenomena. Democracy has been associated with organization of government including institutional arrangements such as elections, party system, and separation of powers. Human rights have been focusing on individual rights and their protection. Furthermore, the organization of government and constitutional arrangements have been considered as an internal matter of the state reflecting sovereignty while human rights have been regarded as universal in scope and subject to international norms and regulations. Finally, academic division of labor between political science—focused on studying democracy—and law and jurisprudence—focused on studying human rights—has magnified these distinctions.

Separation between democracy and human rights, however, is not tenable, because human rights "constitute an intrinsic part of democracy" and the guarantee of basic freedoms is essential for people's voice to be effective in public affairs. On the other hand, one of the basic principles of democracy is popular control over collective affairs, ensuring the right of all citizens to a voice in public affairs. To be effective, this requires appropriate institutional arrangements such as electoral competition between political parties, representative legislature, and independent judiciary through which civil and political rights can be exercised.

The "defining features" of democracy are based on the principles of human rights. The first defining feature—free and fair elections—contributes to political participation and nondiscrimination. Voter education and training, and the exercise of the right to vote increase political legitimacy of the government. The exercise of "people power" through free and fair elections has resulted in new democratic regimes such as in the Philippines, Nigeria, and Malawi. This has strengthened people's right to political participation and nondiscrimination in public affairs.

Second, an elected legislature enhances opportunities for the right to participation and nondiscrimination. . . . Through legislator-constituent interaction, the people have an opportunity to influence the process of lawmaking concerning their civil and political rights as well as enforcement of these laws. The Indian Parliament, for example, has been the most critical forum to raise the issue of discrimination based on language, ethnicity, religion, and regional affiliation. Effectively functioning parliaments also are a mechanism to hold the executive branch accountable for violation of human rights.

Third, independent media promotes the right to the freedom of expression. . . . Media provides a mechanism for the people to express their grievances against the inability or unwillingness of the government machinery to enforce national legislation concerning civil and political rights. In many developing countries, independent and free media plays an important role in making people aware of corrupt practices in the government and exposing the exploitation of vulnerable groups such as children.

Fourth, the separation of powers among different branches of government protects citizens from abuses of their civil and political rights. Where the judiciary is independent, the executive branch is under obligation to provide every citizen due process of law. Similarly, a democratically elected legislature can check the arbitrary exercise of power by the executive. In democratic regimes, the executive branch keeps its professional independence in implementing laws. Thus, the separation of powers provides for a system of checks and balances—protecting the rights of individuals on the one hand and ensuring their fulfillment of obligation on the other.

Fifth, active civil society and a multiparty system—two important features of democracy—promote the right to peaceful assembly and association and thereby ensure accountability of the government. At the national and local levels, civil society organizations and political parties serve as intermediaries to articulate people's aspirations and to hold the institutions of the state accountable to their obligations. Organizations of slum dwellers in the cities of many developing countries have played an important role in changing government policies concerning land regularization and the provision of basic services. International NGOs [non-governmental organizations] such as Amnesty International and Human Rights Watch speak against human rights violations throughout the world. The human rights NGOs use the "power of shame" to encourage state institutions to change their policies and responses; in Brazil, a petition filed by NGOs with the Inter-American Committee on Human Rights resulted in payment of compensation to prisoners' families and new guidelines on the treatment of prisoners based on the UN framework.

Finally, devolution of political authority and resources to local governments provides more opportunities to local citizens to participate in local decision-making process. Where field offices of central government ministries and departments are under direct supervision and control of local governments, elected representatives of the people have an opportunity to take action against abuse of power.

The democratic governance practice in developing economies shows that social injustices—including discrimination against slum dwellers, squatters, migrants, ethnic minorities, and women—are widespread in both democratic and authoritarian regimes. The irony in democratic regimes is that "political incentives to respond to the needs of ordinary people may be offset by incentives to respond to the demands of the powerful or the wealthy." Systematic biases against the poor exist in both types of regimes concerning access to such services as health, education, and shelter. Mali, for example, has made more progress than Togo in strengthening democratic structures but not in elementary education, infant mortality, and literacy. Disparities in income, social advantages, and power exist in both types of regimes. For example, Brazil and the Russian Federation—two of the largest democracies in the world—have some of the widest income disparities, while Indonesia and the Republic of Korea (when under authoritarian rule) achieved significant economic growth but also reduced income disparities.

Democracy and Economic, Social, and Cultural Rights

In many ways, the consolidation and deepening of democracy requires a guarantee of fundamental economic and social rights. The denial of such rights could lead to the inability of those affected to fully exercise their civil and political rights and thus, indirectly, affect the viability of democratic political institutions. The granting of civil and political rights, some argue, might be formalistic for that segment of the population which is characterized by illiteracy, poverty, lack of communication facilities, and dependence upon local landowning groups in rural areas. In such situations, the concerned citizens are not able to exercise their right to hold government officials accountable, even though they might have the right to due process; to have adequate access to justice, even though they have the right to freedom of expression; and to fight against police brutalities, even though there are explicit procedures against such actions.

Two conclusions can be drawn from this. One is that the realization of political and civil rights does not require absolute economic equality among groups; the influence of the wealthy can still be curtailed through such measures as laws that prevent the concentration of media ownership, limit the amount which can be spent on election campaigns, and require sources of the party funding. The second is that all citizens need to have adequate means of livelihoods and income, education, and access to shelter and services such as water, sanitation, and primary health care in order for them to realize their political and social rights. There are, in addition, long-term and indirect consequences of deprivation of basic economic and social rights—the weakening or even breakdown of democratic institutions, urban violence, the displacement of the rural poor and their migration to urban slums and squatter settlements, and eventually the use of excessive force by the state apparatus to deal with political instability.

Democracies must pay attention to the protection of economic and social rights for two major reasons: first, because investment in education, health, and fundamental economic and social rights is the best investment a country can make in its future, and second, because the institutions of a free market economy are vital for the civil society organizations that are central to the sustainability of democracy.

Exclusion, Rights of Minorities, and Inequalities

In democracies, competition for political power and access to power is based in principle on the number of persons supporting a party or individual. The contested issues are usually resolved through the principle of majoritarianism with the assumption that a minority group can be a part of the majority. The rights of minorities are particularly vulnerable where political parties and alliances, and subsequently the outcome of political competition, are based on the ethnicity of regional affiliation. Mistrust among the majority and minority ethnic groups, however, makes such alliances difficult to sustain. Therefore, the rule of the majority has to be reconciled with protection of the fundamental civil, political, and socioeconomic and cultural rights of minorities. For this reason, inclusive democracies provide for the protection of minority groups through specific measures—granting regional autonomy to the minority group, thus making them a majority in their own region; employing a quota system in the composition of the parliament, local government bodies, and executive branch of the government; and instituting various forms of power sharing and affirmative action programs.

In many countries, minorities have been excluded from political participation and their civil and political rights have been violated. Unless democracy is "inclusive," the tendency would be for the majority to increase its power in politics, to question the loyalty of minorities, especially during social stress and economic crisis, to marginalize the language and culture of minorities, and to promote its own interest at the expense of minorities. Violence against minorities is a serious issue even in developed countries, as indicated by attacks, intimidation, and discrimination against immigrants and other minorities in Western Europe.

Inequalities in access to political power and economic resources lead to marginalization and discrimination against minorities. Where leadership of the majority is enlightened, mechanisms are introduced to share economic and political power to ensure the inclusion of minorities. Authoritarian regimes are more likely to abuse the rights of minorities. However, democratic transition would improve the situation of the minorities only if there are specific public policy interventions to protect the rights of minorities. Many countries have recognized the need for special measures to protect and promote the rights of minorities and other disadvantaged groups.

Malaysia, for example, introduced the New Economic Policy (NEP) in 1970s to reduce interethnic disparities in income and assets in order to promote "national unity." The Indian constitution provides for the protection of the rights of lower castes even though serious gaps remain in their implementation. More recently, a [1993] amendment to the constitution has provided for the reservation of one-third of all seats in the Panchayati Raj institutions for women, in order to promote their participation in political decision-making.

Brazil is promoting sustainable development for the indigenous communities in the Amazon region through the improvement of legal protection of their land and the preservation of their cultural heritage. Bolivia, with a large indigenous population, has been implementing a program on the promotion and protection of human rights focused on strengthening institutions, disseminating information, and training public officials engaged in the administration of justice.

Despite the aforementioned examples of the realization of human rights, many democracies in developing and, some would argue in developed countries, harm human rights. This can take many forms—excluding minorities from participation, relocating the minorities from resource rich areas, and failing to establish rule of law. During civil wars, the rights of minorities in democracies are very likely to be violated. Yugoslavia and Sri Lanka are examples. Arbitrary exercise of power in new and restored democracies, especially those with a legacy of military rule, reduces the chances of human rights. Recently, elected governments in Fiji, Sierra Leone, and Ecuador changed because of military and or other unconstitutional means.

Many elected governments in developing countries have not been able to provide universal access to basic services for their populations—the primary indicator of economic and social rights. While this does not justify authoritarian regimes, for example, India, the largest democracy in the world, has not been able to provide the basic service of universal primary education.

Countries with a legacy of authoritarian regimes have taken several measures to protect human rights in the future. Truth and reconciliation commissions have been established to openly discuss the past abuses of human rights, to build national consensus and reconciliation, and to punish the offenders in order to discourage such violations in the future. The National Commission on the Disappearance of Persons in Argentina, and truth and reconciliation commissions in Chile, South Africa, and Uganda are examples. After the end of the military rule, a similar commission was set up in Nigeria as well.

Democracy Does Not Guarantee Human Rights

CNN.com

In the following selection CNN.com, the online counterpart of the international cable news network, discusses a 2006 U.S. State Department report that assessed human rights violations worldwide. According to the report, the worst abuses of human rights occur in nations in which dictators remain unaccountable to their people or to the global community. The State Department, however, also noted that embracing democracy does not necessarily end human rights violations. Several newly formed democracies, for example, are struggling with media and economic freedoms as they seek to prevent social unrest during the transition from tyranny to elected government. Other supposed democracies, the report contends, show signs of backsliding as corruption and despotic leadership thwart attempts at democratic reform.

The State Department on Wednesday [March 8, 2006] said that laudable human-rights practices tend to occur in democracies, but it noted in its annual report on human rights that democracy does not guarantee what President [George W.] Bush has called a commitment to "the non-negotiable demands of human dignity."

Human rights are linked closely to democracies that provide long-term stability and security, said Assistant Secretary for Democracy, Human Rights and Labor Barry Lowenkron, who oversaw the report's compilation.

But, he said, "Some states still have weak institutions of democratic government and continue to struggle; others have yet to commit fully to the democratic process."

CNN.com, "Democracy No Guarantor of Human Rights," March 8, 2006. Reproduced by permission.

The report cited Venezuela and Russia as democratically elected governments that do not always adhere to democratic principles.

The congressionally mandated document—based on reports from governments, multinational institutions, indigenous groups, academics, jurists and the news media—has evaluated the status of individual rights and freedoms since 1977.

The release sparked criticism from Amnesty International, which alleged the United States has "outsourced torture" to some of the countries the report criticizes.

Unaccountable Rulers

The report said countries in which power is concentrated in the hands of unaccountable rulers tend to be the world's most systematic human rights violators. It cited Burma, North Korea. Belarus and Zimbabwe as examples of societies where civil rights are "restricted severely."

"States that severely and systematically violate the human rights of their own people are likely to pose threats to neighbors and the international community," Lowenkron said.

The report cited Iran as a case in point.

"Iran's deprivation of basic rights to its own people, its interference in Iraq, its support for Hezbollah, Hamas and other terrorist organizations, and its refusal to engage constructively on these issues, have further isolated it from the world community," the report said.

Some of the most serious violations of human rights are committed by governments in the context of internal or cross-border conflicts, he said, citing what the United States has termed "genocide" in Sudan.

Where civil societies are under siege, with laws passed or applied against non-governmental organizations and the news media, fundamental freedoms are often undermined, Lowenkron said, citing Zimbabwe, China and Belarus.

China's restrictions on Internet use have had a "chilling effect on freedom of expression, association and assembly," he said.

Progress in Iraq and Afghanistan

Democratic elections tend to put a country on the path to reform, he said, citing last year's elections in Afghanistan and Iraq.

Last year was marked by "major progress for democracy, democratic rights and freedom" in Iraq, the report said, citing the January elections and the growth of NGOs [nongovernmental organizations] and other civil society associations that promote rights.

In Afghanistan, the report noted, September parliamentary elections "occurred against the backdrop of a government still struggling to expand its authority over provincial centers, due to continued insecurity and violent resistance in some quarters."

U.S. allies were not spared. Pakistan's president, Gen. Pervez Musharraf, came under sharp criticism.

"Despite President Musharraf's stated commitment to democratic transition and 'enlightened moderation,' restrictions remained on freedom of movement, expression, association and religion," the report said.

Israel, too, was faulted.

Though the government "generally respected" its citizens' human rights, there were "serious abuses by some members of the security forces against Palestinian detainees," the report said.

About Egypt, which U.S. Secretary of State Condoleezza Rice has visited, Lowenkron said U.S. officials would like the country's political system to open up, "so secular voices will also be heard."

The report cited Syria for refusing to "respect the fundamental freedoms of its people and end its interference in the affairs of its neighbors" by continuing to support terrorist groups and not supporting the U.N. investigation into the murder of Prime Minister Rafiq Hariri of Lebanon.

The report praised Ukraine, Liberia and Lebanon for their democratic transitions and said the Balkans demonstrated "a marked overall improvement in human rights, democracy, and the rule of law over the past several years."

But Uzbekistan's human-rights record, "already poor, worsened considerably in 2005," the report said. It cited the violent uprising in May in the city of Andijon that "led to disproportionate use of force by the authorities and a wave of repressive government actions that dominated the remainder of the year."

Backsliding and Continued Repression

Amid continued concerns about democratic backsliding in Russia, the report said efforts in the country "continued to concentrate power in the Kremlin and direct democracy from the top down."

It singled out Zimbabwe for maintaining "a steady assault on human dignity and basic freedoms, tightening its hold on civil society and human-rights NGOs and manipulating the March parliamentary elections."

And, as it has for years, the report criticized the Cuban government, contending it "continued to control all aspects of life through the communist party and state-controlled mass organizations."

The report said human-rights violations continued in Colombia, though it praised the government's efforts for accountability and said a military offensive has reduced the number of killings and kidnappings.

"In Venezuela, new laws governing libel, defamation and broadcast media content, coupled with legal harassment and physical intimidation, resulted in limitations on media freedoms and a climate of self-censorship," the report said.

Examining Human Rights in the United States

Asked whether the cases of prisoner abuse by U.S. authorities at Abu Ghraib or on Guantanamo had caused the United States to lose the moral high ground on human rights, Lowenkron said they had not.

"This in no way has hindered me from my job, hindered me from my efforts to advance the democratic agenda or the human rights agenda," he said. "If somebody wants to talk about Guantánamo or Abu Ghraib or detainees, I say fine. I'm willing to discuss that with them."

He added that the United States has corrective mechanisms that include "a robust and vigorous press, a Congress that is elected by the people, and an independent judiciary."

Asked about the issue of rendition—in which detainees are sent for questioning to other countries, some of which allow torture—Lowenkron said rendition was done "case-by-case" and only after "we get solid assurances" that the detainees would not be tortured.

The report did not scrutinize human rights in the United States. State Department officials said that the credibility of such a self-review would be questioned, and they noted that independent reviews of U.S. policy are carried out by other entities.

Amnesty International USA was quick to jump into that gap.

"The Bush administration's practice of transferring detainees in the 'war on terror' to countries cited by the State Department for their appalling human rights records actually turns the report into a manual for the outsourcing of torture," said William F. Schulz, the group's executive director.

"The United States government considers itself a moral leader on human rights issues, but its record of indefinite and arbitrary detentions, secret 'black sites' and outsourced torture in the 'war on terror' turns it from leader to human-rights violator."

Globalization Promotes Human Rights

Daniel Griswold

In the following selection Daniel Griswold argues that economic development resulting from globalization leads to increased democracy and respect for human rights. Griswold insists that economic development increases people's access to goods, communication, information, and education. People are therefore less reliant on government to sustain their livelihoods. According to Griswold, having more economic freedoms then prompts people to demand more humanitarian rights and freedoms. This leads Griswold to suggest that the best way to increase human rights around the globe is to increase unrestricted trade and economic development. Daniel Griswold is director of the Center for Trade Policy Studies at the Cato Institute, a libertarian think tank in Washington, D.C.

When trade and globalization are discussed in the U.S. Congress and in the American media, the focus is almost entirely on the economic impact at home—on manufacturing, jobs, and wages. But trade is about more than exporting soybeans and machine tools. It is also about exporting freedom and democracy.

Since September 11, 2001, the [George W.] Bush administration has articulated the argument that trade can and must play a role in promoting democracy and human rights in the rest of the world. In an April 2002 speech, President Bush said, "Trade creates the habits of freedom," and those habits "begin to create the expectations of democracy and demands for better democratic institutions. Societies that are open to commerce across their borders are more open to democracy within their borders."

Daniel Griswold, "Globalization, Human Rights, and Democracy," *eJournalUSA*, February 2006. Reproduced by permission of the author.

Trade, Development, and Political Reform

The connection between trade, development, and political reform is not just a throwaway line. In theory and in practice, economic and political freedoms reinforce one another. Political philosophers from Aristotle to Samuel Huntington have noted that economic development and an expanding middle class can provide more fertile ground for democracy.

Trade and globalization can spur political reform by expanding the freedom of people to exercise greater control over their daily lives. In less developed countries, the expansion of markets means they no longer need to bribe or beg government officials for permission to import a television set or spare parts for their tractor. Controls on foreign exchange no longer limit their freedom to travel abroad. They can more easily acquire tools of communication such as mobile phones, Internet access, satellite TV, and fax machines.

As workers and producers, people in more open countries are less dependent on the authorities for their livelihoods. For example, in a more open, market-driven economy, the government can no longer deprive independent newspapers of newsprint if they should displease the ruling authorities. In a more open economy and society, the "CNN effect" of global media and consumer attention exposes and discourages the abuse of workers. Multinational companies have even greater incentives to offer competitive benefits and wages in more globalized developing countries than in those that are closed.

Economic freedom and rising incomes, in turn, help to nurture a more educated and politically aware middle class. A rising business class and wealthier civil society create leaders and centers of influence outside government. People who are economically free over time want and expect to exercise their political and civil rights as well. In contrast, a government that can seal its citizens off from the rest of the world can more easily control them and deprive them of the resources and information they could use to challenge its authority.

Increased Democratization

As theory would predict, trade, development, and political and civil freedom appear to be tied together in the real world. Everyone can agree that the world is more globalized than it was 30 years ago, but less widely appreciated is the fact that the world is much more democratized than it was 30 years ago. According to the most recent survey by Freedom House [a human rights organization], the share of the world's population enjoying full political and civil freedoms has increased substantially in the past three decades, as has the share of the world's governments that are democratic.

In its annual survey, released in December 2005, the human rights research organization reported that 46 percent of the world's population now lives in countries it classifies as "Free," where citizens "enjoy open political competition, a climate of respect for civil liberties, significant independent civic life, and independent media." That compares to the 35 percent of mankind that enjoyed a similar level of freedom in 1973. The percentage of people in countries that are "Not Free," where political and civil liberties are systematically oppressed, dropped during the same period from 47 percent to 36 percent. The percentage of the population in countries that are "Partly Free" has remained at 18 percent. Meanwhile, the percentage of the world's governments that are democracies has reached 64 percent, the highest in the 33 years of Freedom House surveys.

Thanks in good measure to the liberating winds of globalization, the shift of 11 percentage points of the world's population in the past three decades from "Not Free" to "Free" means that another 650 million human beings today enjoy the kind of civil and political liberties taken for granted in such countries as the United States, Japan, and Belgium, instead of suffering under the kind of tyranny we still see in the most repressive countries.

Within individual countries, economic and political freedoms also appear to be linked. A 2004 study by the Cato Institute, titled "Trading Tyranny for Freedom," found that countries that are relatively open to the global economy are much more likely to be democracies that respect civil and political liberties than those that are relatively closed. And relatively closed countries are far more likely to deny systematically civil and political liberties than those that are open.

From Economic Reform to Political Reform

[Since the 1980s], a number of economies have followed the path of economic and trade reform leading to political reform. South Korea and Taiwan as recently as the 1980s were governed by authoritarian regimes that did not permit much open dissent. Today, after years of expanding trade and rising incomes, both are multiparty democracies with full political and civil liberties. Other countries that have most aggressively followed those twin tracks of reform include Chile, Ghana, Hungary, Mexico, Nicaragua, Paraguay, Portugal, and Tanzania.

In other words, governments that grant their citizens a large measure of freedom to engage in international commerce find it increasingly difficult to deprive them of political and civil liberties, while governments that "protect" their citizens behind tariff walls and other barriers to international commerce find it much easier to deny those same liberties. Of course, the correlation between economic openness and political freedom across countries is not perfect, but the broad trends are undeniable.

The application for U.S. foreign policy is that trade and development, along with its economic benefits, can prove to be powerful tools for spreading broader freedoms and democracy around the world.

In mainland China, for example, economic reform and globalization give reason to hope for political reforms. After

25 years of reform and rapid growth, an expanding middle class is experiencing for the first time the independence of home ownership, travel abroad, and cooperation with others in economic enterprise free of government control. The number of telephone lines, mobile phones, and Internet users has risen exponentially in the past decade. Millions of Chinese students and tourists travel abroad each year. That can only be good news for individual freedom in China, and a growing problem for the government.

Free trade and globalization can also play a role in promoting democracy and human rights in the Middle East. In a May 2003 address outlining his plan for a Middle East free trade area, President Bush said, "The Arab world has a great cultural tradition, but is largely missing out on the economic progress of our time. Across the globe, free markets and trade have helped defeat poverty, and taught men and women the habits of liberty."

Economic stagnation in the Middle East feeds terrorism, not because of poverty but because of a lack of opportunity and hope for a better future, especially among the young. Young people who cannot find meaningful work and who cannot participate in the political process are ripe pickings for religious fanatics and terrorist recruiters. Any effort to encourage greater freedom in the Middle East must include an agenda for promoting economic liberty and openness.

The Future Is Encouraging

On a multilateral level, a successful agreement through the World Trade Organization (WTO) would create a more friendly climate globally for democracy and human rights. Less developed countries, by opening up their own, relatively closed markets and gaining greater access to rich-country markets, could achieve higher rates of growth and develop the expanding middle class that forms the backbone of most democracies. A successful conclusion of the WTO Doha Development Round of trade negotiations that began in 2001 would reinforce the twin trends of globalization and the spread of political and civil liberties that have marked the last 30 years. Failure would delay and frustrate progress on both fronts for millions of people.

[Since the 1970s], globalization, human rights, and democracy have been marching forward together, haltingly, not always and everywhere in step, but in a way that unmistakably shows they are interconnected. By encouraging globalization in less developed countries, we not only help to raise growth rates and incomes, promote higher standards, and feed, clothe, and house the poor; we also spread political and civil freedoms.

Suing Global Corporations Can End Their Human Rights Abuses

Daphne Eviatar

In the following selection Daphne Eviatar uses a legal case against Unocal Corporation, a California-based oil company, to describe how international human rights law is being used to hold corporations accountable for their actions in developing countries. Unocal was found guilty in a U.S. federal court of helping and encouraging the Burmese government to murder and intimidate villagers in order for Unocal to build a gas pipeline on village land. This case, explains Eviatar, has set a precedent, showing other corporations that they will be held responsible for human rights abuses that they encourage or commit. Daphne Eviatar is a freelance writer living in New York City. She has written about international law and development for the New York Times Magazine *and the* Nation.

Early in April [2005], the California-based Unocal Corporation announced it was being bought out by its neighbor, the oil giant ChevronTexaco. Splashed across the business pages, the news overshadowed another announcement, made much more quietly two weeks earlier [in March 2005]: that Unocal had agreed to pay to settle a long-running lawsuit charging the oil company with assisting and encouraging the torture, murder and rape of Burmese villagers by government soldiers so that Unocal could build a gas pipeline. The timing of these two announcements is no coincidence, and it underscores just how seriously these legal cases are now being taken in corporate boardrooms. Once considered mere nuisances,

Daphne Eviatar, "A Big Win for Human Rights," *Nation*, vol. 280, May 9, 2005, pp. 20–22. Copyright © 2005 by The Nation Magazine/The Nation Company, Inc. Reproduced by permission.

lawsuits implicating corporations in international human rights abuses have become major obstacles to corporate profitability and prospects.

Several Suits Are Pending

"Companies like Unocal have been claiming all along that these cases are not to be taken seriously, that they're just brought by a bunch of activists for political reasons without legal grounds, and that no one's had to pay for them and no one ever will," says Katie Redford, a lawyer for EarthRights International, who helped put the case together in 1996 on behalf of one of two groups of Burmese refugees. (Most of the plaintiffs have fled the country and remained anonymous since the case was filed, to protect them from retaliation by the Burmese government) . . . "Companies have been able to mislead themselves and the public that human rights concerns would not affect their bottom line. That's just not the case anymore."

About two dozen cases have been filed against major multinational corporations charging complicity with foreign governments in extraordinary brutality ranging from executions to rape and genocide, usually committed by a foreign military contractually obligated to protect corporate operations. Although about half have been dismissed, usually on procedural grounds, another dozen are still pending. Defendants include some of the largest and most profitable companies in the world: Royal Dutch/Shell, ChevronTexaco, Coca-Cola and ExxonMobil. The Burma case is the first of these to be settled for money damages. Although as a condition of the settlement the size of the payment is confidential, both sides say that the fifteen Burmese villagers who brought the case—each with a unique horror story—won significant monetary compensation. They'll also get money to develop a program to improve the living conditions, healthcare and education of the people who live in the pipeline region, and to help protect them from future abuses. "It's more money than these people will ever know what to do with," says Redford, who just returned from Thailand, where she was visiting the plaintiffs and took some of them shopping for the first time in their lives. "Now they can buy food when they're hungry or medicine when their kids are sick," says Redford. "No one can give them back what they lost, but they wanted this to be a deterrent."

Unocal unwittingly revealed the seriousness of the settlement when in March it boldly sued its insurance companies for the costs of the case. "The allegations of forced labor, murder, rape, torture, battery, forced relocation and detention throughout the Myanmar [modern name of Burma] litigation fall within the policies' 'personal injuries coverage,'" Unocal said in the lawsuit. The insurance companies—which together insured Unocal for up to $60 million in damages—denied the company's claims. That Unocal sued both its primary insurer and its re-insurers, which would only reimburse claims beyond an initial loss of $15 million, makes clear that Unocal's costs were significantly higher than that. Attorneys' fees alone are estimated to have been at least $15 million.

The Unocal Case Sets a New Precedent

But as important as the settlement is the strong legal precedent the Unocal case has set. A series of federal court rulings in California established that a corporation that assists or encourages human rights violations by a foreign government, in this case the Burmese military, can be held legally responsible in a US court. "The standard disclaimers that they've used: that it wasn't our president physically torturing the villagers who worked on the pipeline, it was the government, our joint venture partner, doing this—the Unocal case established that they can't say that anymore," says Jennie Green, a lawyer for the Center for Constitutional Rights who was one of a group of lawyers representing the Burmese villagers.

For years, business groups lobbied hard for repeal of the Alien Tort Claims Act, the law that allowed the suit. The Bush Administration has also taken an unusually strong stand against these cases, intervening several times to ask courts to dismiss them. In the Unocal case Attorney General John Ashcroft filed a brief to the Court of Appeals for the Ninth Circuit denouncing the villagers' attempt to sue under the alien tort law and, in a sweeping argument that surprised even corporate advocates, argued that every court that had allowed these claims in the past twenty years had been wrong. The court rejected his arguments.

But in some ways, the case against Unocal was easy. "This case was unusually well documented," says Harold Hongju Koh, dean of Yale Law School and an expert on human rights law. "Not every case will have that." Indeed, the evidence against the company was damning. Although Unocal repeatedly denied that it knew the Burmese government was using forced labor to clear the land it needed to build the corporation's pipeline, documents revealed that Unocal's consultants had repeatedly warned it of the military's abuses, at one point stating unequivocally that "egregious human rights violations have occurred." The State Department and the United Nations had also denounced the brutality of the Burmese regime.

Businesses Will Be More Careful Abroad

Experts say this case and the settlement will have a broad impact on corporations and force them to consider their conduct overseas. "It puts companies on notice that their relationships with foreign governments, and in particular with foreign militaries, can become the subject of judicial review in the United States," says Elliot Schrage, a former senior vice president of global affairs at the Gap who teaches business strategy and law at Columbia and is a senior fellow at the Council on Foreign Relations. Companies in the extractive industries—oil, gas and mining—will probably be most affected, since they often agree to have a foreign government's armed forces protect company operations.

"Boards of directors are now on notice that this is a governance issue, too," adds Schrage, who believes the settlement was a prerequisite to ChevronTexaco's merger with Unocal. ChevronTexaco itself is now being sued for alleged complicity in a series of shootings and the destruction of two villages by Nigerian military forces protecting its oil operations in the Niger Delta; without a settlement, Unocal would have doubled ChevronTexaco's potential liability for human rights violations and compounded its public embarrassment. Schrage adds that insurance companies will now also scrutinize more closely clients who do business in countries with repressive governments and abusive militaries. The costs of genocide and slavery insurance could be pretty high.

Catherine Boggs, a partner at the international law firm Baker & McKenzie who advises major oil and mining companies on their overseas operations, agrees that the Unocal case has had a real impact. "Companies will give greater weight to this sort of political risk when they consider going into some of these countries, and will be more careful about how they do business with them."

Global Shifts

The recognition that bad corporate conduct overseas can be costly at home is resonating abroad as well. In France, in 2002, Burmese victims sued officials of Total, Unocal's partner in the Burma pipeline and the fourth-largest oil and gas company in the world. And a case against Texaco charging massive environmental contamination in Ecuador is now in trial there. "European corporate lawyers are very worried about such lawsuits," says Menno Kamminga, an international law professor at Maastricht University in the Netherlands, who advises corporations and human rights organizations. "And NGOs [nongovernmental organizations] definitely want to bring them."

But if the movement for legal accountability is slowly going global, so is the pressure to find more oil. World oil consumption is rising dramatically, as is the price per barrel. With countries like China now competing against the major multinationals for drilling rights, the multinationals are under ever greater pressure to pump more oil, more quickly and more cheaply. Historically, that's meant moving into some of the most unstable and politically dicey resource-rich countries in the world.

Ultimately, experts say, only international standards can get all corporations operating overseas to follow the same rules. To that end, the UN is now drafting a set of norms designed to govern transnationai companies. But US officials have already indicated they won't support anything that's enforceable. That leaves the standards to be set by the courts—and at the expense of companies that continue to do big business with bad governments.

The United Nations Promotes Human Rights

Jerry Pubantz

In the following selection Jerry Pubantz argues that the United Nations has created a human rights framework based on democratic process. Different countries and organizations, all with different agendas, meet to discuss and craft human rights. This process, Pubantz says, allows the United Nations to resolve conflict between and within countries without resorting to force. He also argues that human rights at the UN have moved beyond Western conceptions because representatives in the United Nations come from former colonies, poor countries, and nongovernmental organizations. Pubantz describes how the Universal Declaration of Human Rights was drafted via this process and remains a potent measure for addressing human rights concerns. Jerry Pubantz is a professor in the political science department of the University of North Carolina at Greensboro.

Prior to 1945 no international covenant acknowledged human rights or the morality that underpinned those rights as critical elements of peace or as goals to be sought by sovereign national governments. Even the UN Charter, which includes seven references to human rights, was not crafted with individual or communal rights as a central preoccupation of the United Nations. Rather, the new United Nations was meant to maintain peace through the concerted political and military effort of the world's great powers. However, between the UN's founding and the current moment, the world community has created panoply of rights, largely through UN institutional structures. UN Secretary General Kofi Annan (2005) affirmed the centrality of human rights to global security and to the

Jerry Pubantz, "Constructing Reason: Human Rights and the Democratization of the United Nations," *Social Forces*, vol. 84, December 2005, pp. 1291–1300. Copyright © 2005 by The University of North Carolina Press. Used by permission.

work of the United Nations in sweeping reform proposals made in the spring of 2005. His actions marked an extraordinary evolution of the world organization, a new conceptualization of the prerequisites for world peace, and an opportunity for individuals and non-state organizations to influence the expanding international human rights regime.

A new international governance structure has emerged in the past two decades that provides extensive points of influence for nongovernmental organizations (NGOs), socially progressive movements and individuals. Through the network of intergovernmental organizations created since World War II, assisted by the process of globalization, internet communication, media saturation and concentrations of financial resources, private actors can affect international agenda-setting, decision-making and policy implementation in many areas of global governance. Human rights creation has been one of the arenas of thematic diplomacy in which national governments have had to cede their monopoly over international negotiation, allowing a more democratized process that in turn lends itself to increased legitimacy for the universal rights created. The steady democratization of the United Nations system has produced what [political theorist] Jürgen Habermas identifies as a "rationally justified consensus" on what constitutes universal human rights in the new millennium, thus contributing to the resolution of inter-state and intra-state conflict without the resort to force. . . .

Somewhere between the facts of state-dominated international politics and the norms of a universal human rights regime lies the burgeoning discursive politics of contemporary international organization. While the UN system is surely not what Habermas would call a "cosmopolitan democracy," it has served as the primary forum for global human rights formation. In the deliberative process of UN negotiation disparate actors—national government representatives, individual activists, NGOs and other international organization delegates and bureaucrats—craft human rights and attempt to extrapolate them to real life experience. . . .

Creating Universal Standards

From its earliest moments the United Nations offered a practical avenue for human rights advocates pursuing their agenda. Many delegates to the 1945 San Francisco Conference hoped the UN Charter would enshrine an international bill of human rights. Newly independent nations pressed for charter commitments on decolonization, economic and social issues, and human rights. Under the influence of domestic religious, civic, labor and libertarian organizations, the American delegation to the San Francisco Conference also urged that the charter contain language promoting human rights and the formal recognition of a consultative role for nongovernmental organizations.

In the UN's formative years the human rights effort was closely associated with the work of former First Lady Eleanor Roosevelt. She chaired the first meetings of the UN Commission on Human Rights (CHR), which authored the Universal Declaration of Human Rights. She and others believed it would be too difficult to bridge the cross-cultural and ideological differences among national delegations on a formal human rights treaty, and therefore she proposed the drafting of a universal declaration with persuasive moral value that could be signed well ahead of binding conventions. Working with a group of celebrated international legal minds from a variety of cultures, including Chinese philosopher Peng-chung Chang, Hernán Santa Cruz from Chile, and the Latin American political left, Hansa Mehta from India (who insisted that women's equality be clearly articulated), and René Cassin, a French Jew with an outlook colored by the most recent and appalling example of human rights violations, Roosevelt discovered that conceptualizing rights and fleshing out international law were multicultural, even multi-civilizational endeavors. When, in late 1948, the General Assembly passed the Universal Declaration without a dissenting vote, no longer could it be asserted without challenge that the notion of rights was strictly a Western conceit. . . .

Moving Beyond Political Rights

Eighteen years after passage of the Universal Declaration and the Convention on Genocide, the General Assembly opened for signature the International Covenant on Economic, Social and Cultural Rights (ICESCR), and the International Covenant on Civil and Political Rights (ICCPR). Both came into force in 1976, and together with the Universal Declaration made up the "International Bill of Human Rights" sought by so many at the time of the UN's founding.

The ICESCR is particularly important because it marks a departure from liberalism's emphasis on individual political and juridical rights. It acknowledges as "rights" those things that in the west are more usually understood as social and economic "benefits" obtained through policy choices in a domestic society. The ICESCR provides guarantees of "the right of everyone to the enjoyment of an adequate standard of living for himself and his family, including adequate food, clothing and housing, and to the continuous improvement of living conditions." It also guarantees access to adequate education, social security, medical care, employment, shelter, mental health and leisure, requiring an expansion of governmental functions. The covenant, by the nature of the rights it identifies, establishes under international law elements of economic and social development as fundamental human rights. This principle was given practical meaning in the Millennium Development Goals (MDGs) approved by the Millennium Summit in 2000. The summit committed the world community to reduce by half the number of people living on $1 a day and those who suffer from hunger or live without sustainable access to safe drinking water; to eliminate gender disparity in education and society as a whole; and to reduce by two-thirds the mortality rate of children under the age of 5 by significant improvements to maternal health aimed at reducing the maternal mortality rate by 75 percent. The UN set the year 2015 as the deadline for achieving MDG targets and for halting and then beginning to reverse the spread of HIV/AIDS, malaria and other major diseases. . . .

Making the Global Community Responsible

In the summer of 1993 the United Nations convened the World Conference on Human Rights, also known as the Vienna Conference. The 171 participating nations adopted a declaration affirming the principle that "all human rights are universal," and that "it is the duty of states, regardless of their political, economic and cultural systems, to promote and protect all human rights and fundamental freedoms." The Vienna Declaration and Program of Action highlighted the links among development, democracy and the promotion of human rights. It emphasized the indivisibility and interdependence of civil, cultural, economic, political and social rights, declaring all to be the responsibility of governments and requiring governments to promote all human rights and fundamental freedoms. The declaration reaffirmed the right to development as a universal, inalienable, integral and fundamental part of human rights. The signatories of the Vienna Declaration agreed that the development of the poorest nations was the collective responsibility of the international community. The Final Document asserted that extreme poverty and social exclusion constituted a "violation of human dignity." The declaration emphasized the rights of all vulnerable groups, especially women, and extended this protection to indigenous peoples.

The Vienna Conference and subsequent Millennium Summit in 2000 were watershed events in the creation of human rights. The latter gathering established a new standard—personal sovereignty—as a guiding principle of international affairs. In his address and report to the Summit, Secretary General Annan reminded the world that the charter opens with the words, "We the *Peoples*," not "We the *States*." He noted that the charter "reaffirms the dignity and worth of the human person, respect for human rights and the equal rights of men and women, and a commitment to social progress ... in freedom from want and fear alike. Ultimately, then, the United Nations exists for, and must serve, the needs and hopes of people everywhere. . . . No shift in the way we think or act can be more critical than this: we must put people at the centre [*sic*] of everything we do." . . .

Summit participants agreed on six "fundamental values" essential to international relations: freedom, equality, solidarity, tolerance, respect for nature and a sense of shared responsibility. These were values of a new era in international politics, potentially inherent in the UN Charter, but never at the heart of the day-to-day diplomacy within the international organization. The declaration set specific goals that combined development, democratization and human rights. As the world's conflicts shifted from Cold War causes to religious, ethnic and economic origins in the developing world, the United Nations shifted its activity. Particularly through the nexus of nation-building, human rights and development, the UN sought to address the overwhelming internal problems of states at risk, raise the standard of living for millions, and promote international stability by ending human right abuses within countries. . . .

Successful UN Programs

[Since the 1980s] peacekeeping interventions in Namibia, Cambodia, Somalia, Congo, Kosovo, Timor-Leste, Bosnia and other paralyzed states have emphasized the promotion of human rights and democracy. The UN role has included election-monitoring; reconstruction of legal systems; creation of civil society organizations; constitutional reform; protection and political advancement of women, indigenous peoples and minority groups; economic development; and the enhancement of social justice. The United Nations had particular electoral success in El Salvador, East Timor, Mozambique, Cambodia, Guatemala and Angola. No longer sufficient to restore peace between contending forces, the UN also provided a transitional administration. In Annan's words, "inevitably that means political institutions. At the center of virtually every civil war is the issue of the state and its power—who controls it, and how it is used. No armed conflict can be resolved without responding to those questions. Nowadays the answers almost always have to be democratic ones." The United Nations' state-building initiatives included the protection of opposition factions, the political mobilization of often marginalized groups such as women and indigenous peoples, and the restoration or creation of judicial institutions in order to assure the rule of law and the defense of individual liberties. . . .

Partnerships with Nongovernmental Organizations

Nation-building and the successful attainment of the MDG targets are largely dependent . . . on NGO [nongovernmental organization] engagement, both in the policy-making process and in the implementation of international efforts locally. The United Nations can only achieve its goals through partnerships with civil society on the international, national and subnational levels. The United Nations must work not only with the governments that are its members but also with the nonstate actors that are so much a part of contemporary global affairs.

Article 71 of the UN Chapter urges the Economic and Social Council (ECOSOC) to grant "consultative status" to nongovernmental organizations that are involved with issues addressed by the United Nations. In the late 1980s and 1990s, NGO participation in the United Nations grew dramatically. . . . NGOs have become "citizen organizations" within the United Nations, advocating particular goals and mobilizing support for UN initiatives. They are Habermas's "nodal points" in the international communications network, part of international civil society, advancing the salient issues, possible solutions and constructed values of a vibrant democratic process into the public sphere where global consensus formation is possible.

In 1996 ECOSOC took a seminal step, passing Resolution 31, giving NGOs expanded access to the council. Those granted "General" consultative status were allowed observers at ECOSOC meetings and permitted to submit written statements to both the council and subsidiary bodies. They could also address the council on subjects of interest. As a result, these organizations regularly circulated materials to member-state offices in New York City and Geneva, Switzerland, providing an opportunity for enhanced interest group advocacy. . . .

UN human rights bodies are assisted by a large number of nongovernmental organizations that serve as advocates of human rights and work to protect them. At times the NGOs intervene to protect individuals who are denied their rights. These NGOs monitor the situation in each of the world's nations and submit informative reports to the various monitoring bodies. Among the most influential in the UN policy process are Amnesty International and Human Rights Watch. Nearly all UN human rights committees actively solicit NGO participation. Materials submitted by nongovernmental organizations are regularly distributed to committee members. Each committee, depending on its specific rules of procedure, allows NGOs to address the plenary session, working groups or informal sessions of the body. . . .

A Reformulated Agenda

In April 2005, Annan spoke to the opening session of UN Commission on Human Rights, meeting in Geneva. He used the occasion to promote his latest reform proposal to replace the commission with a smaller, but more authoritative, Human Rights Council. He reminded the commission that its membership and activities had not been without controversy, particularly as members often had questionable human rights records of their own. He also forwarded the thesis that human rights could not be assured without a concurrent commitment to development and international security, nor could the latter two be guaranteed without a global commitment to human rights.

This tripartite formulation of security, development and human rights provides the foundation for the latest UN reform proposals urged by Annan in his 2005 report entitled *In Larger Freedom*. Well known for its endorsement of an enlarged Security Council, a new Peacebuilding Commission and a redefinition of collective security in the 21st century, the secretary general's program also insists the world community provide freedom from want, freedom from fear, and protection for those abused by their own governments. Only the full engagement of international civil society by a reformed United Nations can make these rights secure.

The UN Human Rights Commission Should Not Admit Human Rights Violators to Its Membership

Frida Ghitis

In the following article Frida Ghitis argues that countries with records of human rights violations should not be allowed to be members of the United Nations Human Rights Commission (UNHRC). She explains that the UNHRC claims to set the standard for human rights policy but that the commission undercuts its authority as long as it admits human rights violators into its ranks. Countries that are members of the UNHRC despite records of human rights abuse include Sudan and Zimbabwe. Ghitis calls for a reform of the UNHRC that includes minimum human rights standards for membership. Frida Ghitis is a contributor to the Jewish World Review *and the* New Republic. *She is also author of* The End of Revolution: A Changing World in the Age of Live Television.

It is time once again to mock the victims of human rights abuse. Yes, it is time for the yearly session of the United Nations Commission on Human Rights, the group that describes itself as the "world's foremost human rights forum" and, with no trace of irony, dares to declare that it "continues to set the standards that govern the conduct of states."

In reality, the commission has become the clearest symbol of the UN's need to change. Today, it represents little more than a gruesome caricature of what started in the earliest days of the United Nations as an earnest effort to ensure respect for the rights of every individual on the planet.

Frida Ghitis, "The UN Charade on Human Rights," *Boston Globe*, March 27, 2005, p. K11. Reproduced by permission of the author.

To get an idea of the panel's moral authority, picture a project to combat crime featuring Jeffrey Dahmer and Charles Manson on its top commission.

And yet, this 61st annual session presents the world with the ideal opportunity to take constructive action. The UN Human Rights body is such a travesty that even the UN's staunchest supporters know it cries out for reform. Critics and supporters of the UN must seize this moment, with the spotlight on this preposterous organization, to work together on a solution. And the solution must include minimum standards for membership.

Human Rights Violators on the Commission

During the six weeks from March 14 until April 22 [2005], members of the 53-country commission will gather in Geneva and pretend to protect human rights. Those seated at the table, looking serious and committed to the cause, will include a Who's Who of perpetrators of large-scale crimes against their own people.

The commission this year includes countries like Sudan, whose government, much of the world agrees, is complicit in the murder of tens of thousands and the forced displacement of millions of the country's citizens. A UN report found the government and its allies guilty of carrying out a policy of murdering, raping, torturing, and destroying the villages of non-Arab Sudanese in the Darfur region of the country. The world can't quite agree on whether Sudan's government is guilty of genocide or crimes against humanity. Yet Sudan's representative will help "set the standards" for human rights around the world.

Sudan will receive presumably invaluable help in its efforts to protect human rights from the government of Zimbabwe, whose president used battalions of thugs to intimidate the opposition, destroy freedom of the press, and successfully destroy the country's economy, plunging most of its population into poverty. They will work shoulder to shoulder with that other defender of freedom, equality, and tolerance: Saudi Arabia.

Monarchs, despots, and dictators of all stripes will contribute to the commission's work, with regime representatives from such paragons of human rights as Cuba, Nepal, Egypt, Pakistan, Swaziland, Bhutan, and China, among others, helping craft the agenda to defend human rights and individual freedoms around the world.

Just wait until you see their work. They will attack the actions of democracies and they will do their best to prevent any resolution that tarnishes the image of the panel's members or their friends.

The commission is an insult to the millions of people who have fled their homes running from slaughter and now live in squalid refugee camps in places like Chad, Sudan, and Congo. It is an affront to the hundreds of millions of women treated as second-class citizens and abused with the consent of their governments in dozens of countries around the world. It mocks the struggle of millions in the Middle East and other parts of Asia, Africa, and even parts of Europe, who want to share the freedoms others take for granted in much of the world.

The gathering of what is supposed to be the world's principal body for protecting human rights should bring hope to the oppressed around the world. Instead, it sinks their spirits. What could be more discouraging than seeing your oppressors treated as honorable members of that, of all commissions?

The time is long overdue for the UN's human rights charade to come to an end. How best to honor the victims than to do some thorough spring-cleaning? Scrub the UN Human Rights Commission of human rights violators and other despots.

Membership on the commission should constitute a high honor. Only those who deserve it should have a seat at the table.

The Internet Can Help Improve Human Rights

Lloyd Axworthy

In the following selection Lloyd Axworthy argues that the Internet can be a powerful tool for benefiting human rights. Axworthy says that the Internet allows greater civic participation within a nation. It also keeps insiders and foreign interest groups aware of potential human rights abuses so that responsive measures can be organized. However, Axworthy warns that the Internet cannot remain unregulated because it is also a tool that can be used to foster human rights violations. The author concludes that in order for the Internet to promote human rights, more people must have access to it. Lloyd Axworthy is director and CEO of the Liu Centre for the study of global issues at the University of British Columbia in Canada.

Grand Chief Phil Fontaine, the head of Canada's Assembly of First Nations, once gave me a wonderful gift—a talking stick. It is a technology that goes back thousands of years—for when handed to the user it is supposed to imbue the speakers' words with courage, honesty and wisdom—not always guaranteed, alas, because that depends on the person holding the stick. For our First Nations people it carries great significance and responsibility—when the stick is in your hand—there is the power to speak straight—to communicate what is good—to help in the search of truth.

Today's electronic, wired cyberspace technology can also be a talking stick that can bring with it the capacity to speak straight—to contribute to the common good, to advance the cause and commitment to human rights. The key is how to

Lloyd Axworthy, "The Mouse Is Mightier than the Sword," in *Human Rights and the Internet*. Hampshire, UK: St. Martin's Press, 2000. © 2000 Macmillan Press Ltd. Reproduced with permission of Palgrave Macmillan.

maximize the Internet's potential for good as a tool to promote and protect human rights: its use for human rights education, as a means of organizing human rights defenders and getting information on human rights violations out to the world. This is a technology that is revolutionizing the world. It is changing the equations of power, challenging the conventional channels of communication, distributing and disseminating influence in the broadest possible fashion. It is democratizing the channels—and getting rid of the gatekeepers.

The issue that is posed is to what end—for what purpose; for as with most technologies there is the potential for evil as well as good. For all the opportunity it represents, there is a dark side. An international operation under INTERPOL [an international police agency] arrested in one week over 100 people in 12 countries involved in a child pornography ring. Racists and extremists use the Net to incite hate. The drug dealers and the crime rings turn the Internet to their advantage—using it to help overturn governments and corrode society. So part of the human rights and Internet question is how to prevent the abuse of this technology.

The Internet Should Not Be a Law-Free Zone

The information superhighway can transport the best but it can also transport the worst. Hate speech, child pornography and child prostitution have moved onto the Net and they have to be dislodged. The aim is not to control the Internet *per se* —but to take aim at those who would misuse it for criminal and other illegal activities which can hurt or harm. The Internet should not be a law-free zone. We are working with other governments, through the OECD [Organization for Economic Co-operation and Development], the G8 [Group of 8 countries Canada, France, Germany, Italy, Japan, Russia, the United Kingdom, and the United States, that hold an annual political and economic Summit], the UN and other international organizations, to prevent the Internet from becoming a safe haven for conduct which threatens human rights. Canadian courts and legislatures are acknowledged to have done groundbreaking work in defining when freedom of expression must give way to criminal law sanctions for obscenity, hate propaganda and child pornography. Our experience in the real world could guide us in addressing similar challenges in the cyber world—where the consequences of hurtful actions are no less destructive.

In addition to better enforcement of domestic and international criminal laws, other means are being developed to address harmful and illegal content on the Net, including self-regulation, software filtering, voluntary codes of conduct and various forms of Internet watch activities to protect consumers and children. For example, in January 1999, Canada participated in an international meeting of officials and experts on child pornography convened by UNESCO [United Nations Educational, Scientific and Cultural Organization] in Paris, to coordinate a worldwide offensive against paedophile activity and materials on the Net. The conference developed a Declaration and Action Plan directed at providing a safe environment for children on the Internet through cooperation among governments, international organizations, law enforcement agencies, families, educators and the media.

The newly minted statute of the International Criminal Court has helped give definition to a range of international crimes and a mechanism to enforce the international Rule of Law. The Internet offers a potentially powerful way to make the most of this new instrument. By disseminating information on the court's objectives and as a channel to gain support for the Court's work, by providing access and links to sites with key documents, such as the International Law Website, or by possibly providing a cyber forum where experts can assist the ICC from their own desktops, the Internet can extend the reach and ensure the effectiveness of the Court.

Thus there is a serious agenda on how to ensure that today's talking stick is not used to foment hate and exploitation but is used to support those working against these things. Yet we should not be overly preoccupied with the dark side of the Internet because the potential of this technology to break through barriers, overcome political obstacles—to educate, inform and to be an agent of political change—boggles the mind. Putting information and communication technologies to the service of human needs means developing ways to deal with harmful and illegal uses, but we must take care to do so without destroying those very attributes that make these technologies such a powerful tool for human rights advocacy in the first place.

The Internet Can Be a Tool of Democracy

The revolution in communications and information technology is taking place at the same time as two other global trends are emerging: increasing democratization and the growing importance of global governance. One of the key questions in this debate is how we can link these three trends. Information technology is reorganizing international politics, giving power and influence to the disenfranchized, empowering new groups and rewriting the constellation of international players. The Internet is an unparalleled tool in a complex world where soft power—influencing events using attractive ideas, promoting shared values and partnership—is emerging as a way of pursuing our goals. I have seen first hand the power of the new communications in the landmines campaign, where the Internet gave international civil society a new say in pushing forward shared objectives. Clearly, the new information and communications technologies are an instrument for change. Our concern here is how to use them to achieve our goals of more democratic societies, and better governance, and with respect for the rule of human rights law.

Democratization does not happen simply by holding elections. Democratization requires an active, effective civil society. It requires citizens who are ready, willing and able to participate in the political life of their country, and who are not only permitted but also encouraged to do so. The Internet has the potential to shelter and nourish opposition groups who are seeking democratic change under repressive regimes. It can help overcome the monopolies of state-controlled media. Governments are still coming to grips with this new phenomenon—some are not yet able to fully comprehend it and some are reacting out of fear, hopelessly trying to seal off populations from the connection and influence of the Net—frankly to little avail.

In new democracies, the Net can increase democratic awareness and popular participation. Canada has supported the establishment of an electronic conferencing service which links up parliamentarians from nine South African provinces. This project is part of our efforts to help South Africa rebuild and reform its post-apartheid governance institutions.

The Internet also allows human rights defenders to educate, organize and get information about human rights violations out to the international community at the tap of a cursor. The reports of the UN Special Rapporteurs, including the Special Rapporteur on Freedom of Opinion and Expression—a Canadian initiative—are now widely available on the Net. This helps the international community track violations and marshal condemnation of governments who violate the human rights of their citizens. The website of the UN High Commissioner for Human Rights allows complaints of human rights violations to be instantly transmitted to Geneva, where the human rights treaty bodies and rapporteurs can take urgent action to prevent further violations. Dozens of Internet mailing lists, web pages, Usenet groups and other tools are springing up around the world to track human rights abuses. Urgent appeals and public campaigns in response to violations can be received instantly—and can prevent further abuses. When the interest of major television media has cooled and moved on, the Internet can help keep the heat on—focusing international attention on ongoing human rights abuses. We can take as a concrete example the winter of 1996 when Serbian students, protesting the government's refusal to respect election results, circumvented state controls on the media by operating a website to get news to the Serbian and international community.

More People Should Have Internet Access

The potential of the Internet is limited only by the number of people who are able to take advantage of it. The Internet can only be a truly universal instrument for human rights if it is both equitable and accessible. Equity and accessibility are closely linked. Universal access, including targeted measures for marginalized groups, must be central to our efforts. If the Net is to serve human rights, it has to reach both urban and rural communities, developing and industrialized countries, women and men.

The Net will only be a half-developed tool if it fails to respond to the needs of half the world's population. We saw, during preparations for the Beijing Fourth World Conference on Women, women's groups from the North and the South forging links over the Net, exchanging information, establishing coalitions and building bridges. Young people, among the most active Internet users, are also applying their energy and imagination to ensuring universal access. The Youth International Internship Programme (YIIP), has supported the training of developing country NGOs [non-governmental organizations] in the uses of the Internet. Since 1997, over 100 young Canadians have worked with human rights organizations, many helping to provide them with technological training including website creation, Internet research methodology and electronic publishing.

The Internet Is a Powerful Human Rights Tool

The examples I have cited demonstrate the power of the Internet to move the cause of human rights ahead. But they are just the beginning. We should continue to look for other ways to build on these successes. Recognizing that human rights defenders, students and other members of civil society needed better access to information on human rights norms and situations around the world, in 1997 we entered into a partnership with Human Rights Internet (a Canadian NGO) to produce an annual report entitled *For the Record: the UN Human Rights System*. The project's goal was, and continues to be, to make the vast quantity of UN human rights documents more accessible. By bringing together all UN information on human rights themes and specific country situations, *For the Record* has proven to be a valuable research and advocacy tool, demonstrating that the Internet can be used constructively to improve our lives by promoting human rights.

We are seeing that the Internet can be a powerful tool for human rights. Where human rights organizers once spent time clipping newspaper articles and organizing phone trees, now communication can be instantaneous and universal. International human rights standards can be made available to children around the world to help foster a global culture of human rights. Governments can use the Net to work in partnership with non-governmental organizations to provide human rights expertise and technical assistance. In this way, the Internet can work to close the gap between international human rights standards and practice on the ground. As a result, the 19th-century adage 'the pen is mightier than the sword', can perhaps be updated for the 20th and 21st century to read, 'the mouse is mightier than the missile'.

These are extremely complex questions—how can the Internet be used as a positive force for human rights—for advocacy, awareness and urgent action in response to violations—

while guarding against its use as a tool to spread hate? I am under no illusions about the difficulty of the issues facing us, in conceptual, legal and practical terms. But today's information and communications technology has enormous potential to move the human rights agenda forward. We have only glimpsed the possibilities and begun to take some first, small steps. With further imagination and ingenuity we can certainly transform this technology into the new millennium's talking stick.

CHAPTER 4

Personal Perspectives on Human Rights Issues

The Plight of Refugees from Liberia's Civil War

Caroline Moorehead

In the selection that follows Caroline Moorehead shares the testimony of a Liberian refugee named Musa Sherif, whom she met in Cairo in 2000. In 1999 Sherif escaped from Liberia, a country in western Africa embroiled in a brutal civil war. However, according to Musa's account, life was not easy for refugees in Cairo. Musa and many other refugees were stranded in the foreign city where they could not get regular jobs because they had not achieved citizenship. As Moorehead explains, the process of gaining asylum was slow and frustrating. The refugees Moorehead met in Cairo are forced to suffer these circumstances even though the Universal Declaration of Human Rights promises all people the right to safety and security, the right to asylum in other countries, the right to work, and the right to enjoy a healthy standard of living. Moorehead explains that hope for Musa and the other refugees was entirely in the hands of the bureaucratic United Nations High Commission for Refugees, which has the power to grant them amnesty. Caroline Moorehead writes about human rights issues for the Times *and the* Independent, *two UK newspapers. She also has made TV programs for the British Broadcasting Corporation (BBC) about human rights.*

I met Musa Sherif for the first time in the late afternoon of February 5, 2000. . . . It was my first day in Cairo. I wouldn't have noticed him, for he was one of fifty-six young Liberians gathered in the office of the African Studies department of the American University in Cairo, had it not been for his pressed, almost starched new trousers. He was also the only young man in a tie. Later, I would see him in very clean denim dun-

Caroline Moorehead, from *Human Cargo: A Journey Among Refugees*. New York: Henry Holt, 2005. © 2005 Caroline Moorehead. Reprinted by permission of Henry Holt and Company, LLC. In the United Kingdom by Random House Ltd.

garees, and in a baggy green suit of trousers and bomber
jacket, in a fashionable military color, with striking emerald
green leather sneakers: clothes, for Musa, as for many of the
young men, were a symbol of possibility, of belief that there
was some order in a profoundly disordered world, and still
some hope of being able to make an impression on it.

A Community of Refugees

On this afternoon in early February, Musa had followed the
other young men to a meeting called by Barbara Harrell-
Bond, who, as emeritas professor in refugee studies at the
American University, long a defender and protector of refugees, had become a point of reference for asylum seekers in
Cairo. They were sitting on the floor, pressed closely together
because the office was too small for such gatherings, in a
room of faded elegance, with ornate latticed doors and deco-
rated tiles, remnants of Cairo's earlier grandeur. Musa was one
of the young men who spoke. His English was good and his
voice clear and precise. With his shirt and tie, and his overly
big glasses with their round frames, he had the look of a
bookish, eager accountant or librarian. What I didn't then
know was that Musa had been a schoolteacher until the nightmare of his current life overtook him, and that, as the brightest and most promising in a large family of sons, he had been
selected by his father as the one to study and make his way in
a world beyond their farm and village. Nor did I know then
that peculiar-looking little Abdullai, with his bright pink
woman's quilted jacket and children's furry earmuffs, to which
were attached wire antennae, which quivered as he moved his
head, was not yet fifteen, and living in a derelict car abandoned beyond the airport, and that he was often hungry; or
that Abdularam, sitting cross-legged in the front row and asking a stream of highly technical questions about the Refugee

Convention,[1] spoke such unfathomable English because he had no back teeth on either side, from years of violence and neglect. Later, all these Liberians would become real people to me, as I carried their stories around with me in my head, stories of murdered parents and burned-out homes, tales of terror and flight, and as I slowly pieced together, fragment by fragment, from meetings or calls late at night from public telephone boxes and offered tentatively as bits in a vast, uncompleted jigsaw, the map of each one's particular odyssey. In the same way, later, Liberia itself would become a real place for me, a country of rivers and mountains and towns, but also a place of war and violence, with its military commanders, its rebel checkpoints, and its random, hideous brutality. Unschooled, for the most part on the run and lost for several years, these young men turned out to be keen historians of the civil wars that had destroyed their families and their childhoods.

That late afternoon in February, as the winter sun went down, and the light in the small cramped room faded, and the noises from the narrow street of car repair shops and spare parts outside began to grow faint, the Liberians talked on and on, about themselves and their fears about what was happening to them. It marked a particular moment in the lives of these fifty-two young men and four young women. Until that afternoon, these young people had been drifting along the margins of Cairo's immense refugee population in search of help, teaming up sometimes, like Musa, with another asylum seeker from another African country, but for the most part totally alone. After this time, they would become a band, with the rivalries and animosities inevitable among people so anxious and so destitute, but a band nonetheless, looking after the interests of the others, so that when Abudu was the first to

1. The Convention Relating to the Status of Refugees was adopted in 1951 to provide international protection for refugees. The international convention defines who is a refugee, the rights of refugees, and the responsibilities of nations granting asylum. It was approved at a UN conference on July 28, 1951.

be accepted for resettlement in the United States, and Amr went to prison on obscure charges of spying for Israel, these events would be personal in the life of each of them. . . .

Musa's Story

Among the young Liberians, Musa is remarkable only for the remorselessness of the horrors that overtook him. His father was a prosperous Mende farmer in Grand Capemount County, with four wives. Musa, the brightest boy in the family, was sent away to Sierra Leone to train to become a teacher. He was a studious boy and he learned good English and Arabic. When he was seventeen, he went home to teach in the local school and prepare to succeed his father as village elder. In a photograph taken at the time, which he has carried with him all these years, he looks absurdly small and young. He is a short, stocky young man, with a very round face and an almost jaunty manner. Musa was at home, in the large family compound, with his pregnant new wife, sixteen-year-old Zainab, when in 1997 Charles Taylor's[2] second wave of civil war brought marauding killers to Grand Capemount County. Taylor's soldiers wanted no elders and no educated Mendes in the new Liberia. The killing was slow and deliberate. First the women and the girls, after raping them; then the elders, using machetes to chop off arms and legs; then the young men, shot with Kalashnikovs [AK-47 rifles]. Musa, in a line with four of his brothers, was the last. By the time the soldiers reached him, an officer had arrived. The killing was stopped. His brothers were all dead, along with his mother, father, and sisters. Musa was alive.

He fled. Three days later, at the border with Sierra Leone, he found Zainab; she had been raped twice but had not lost the baby. They crossed the frontier and wandered in the bush, eating grass and roots, with Zainab's mother and a little girl of

---

2. Taylor was a warlord and leader of the National Patriotic Front of Liberia during the civil war from 1989–1996 and president of Liberia from 1997–2003.

five, found abandoned along the way, whose parents had been murdered in front of her. One day rebels—bands of soldiers roamed both sides of the border—caught Musa's mother-in-law as she was gathering berries; they raped and mutilated her, and, in great pain, she died. Then Musa was captured, slapped about, scarred with the blade of a bayonet. But Zainab hid in the bushes with the little girl; Zainab's baby, a boy, was born under a tree soon afterward and survived. Musa escaped and found them and they pressed on, hiding in the undergrowth, begging food from villagers. At last they reached a refugee camp, but they were turned away: it was full, and those who ran it by now feared that all young Liberian men might be killers with tribal scores to settle.

So they wandered on, stopping from time to time to rest, until one day, on the outskirts of Liberia's capital, Monrovia, they met a friend of Musa's father, a Lebanese trader. The friend, knowing that Musa could not survive for long in a country run by Charles Taylor's men—who were then hunting down all they suspected of being rebel fighters—brought him a plane ticket and a visa for Egypt. Zainab, their son, their adopted daughter, and a new second baby found refuge with an aunt. Musa was now twenty-two. In Egypt, he believed that he would find asylum; the United Nations High Commissioner for Refugees—UNHCR—would surely grant him refugee status and bring his wife and children to join him. He flew to Cairo, expectant, exhausted by months of fear, frantic with worry about his family.

Life in Cairo

That was in 1999. By the time I reached Cairo in February 2000, Musa was still alone, stateless, without papers, work, a home, or his family. UNHCR had neither interviewed him nor recognized his claim to be a refugee. He had lost touch with Zainab and the children; he believed they had fled over the border into Guinea, where the camps for those who escape Liberia's continuing carnage are renowned for rape and casual murder. The politics of the modern refugee world are not on Musa's side, chiefly because he arrived in Egypt too late. By 1999, all Africa seemed to be on the move, running from the civil wars that to this day consume the continent, while many other desperate people had been drawn north by Egypt's open-door policy, not knowing that the country had neither the means of looking after those they so hospitably allowed in, nor any intention of doing so, and that the rest of the world had few plans to give them refuge, either.

Over the next three years, shocked by what he felt to be betrayal, Musa slowly shed his hopes. He accepted that he had nowhere to sleep, but had to move from week to week to the floors of other refugees' rooms, always hiding, knowing that if he was picked up by the police without papers he might be deported or imprisoned. He had understood that he would still have to wait, perhaps for years, for UNHCR to decide whether what he witnessed and endured amounted to the "justified fear of persecution" that would alone grant him refugee status and the possibility of resettlement in the West. He had accepted that he would find no work other than occasional day labor in the black economy, for as an asylum seeker with no papers he could not officially work. He concentrated only on one thing: finding his wife and children and bringing them to live with him on the streets of Cairo. (It was not until much later, when I went to the border between Liberia, Sierra Leone, and Guinea, that I really understood why the young Liberians had known that they had to flee.) Among the small community of Liberian lost boys, he was seen as a loner; he preferred to put his energy into his dreams, alongside which Cairo, with its overcrowding and its incessant noise, its poverty and racism, its bullying police and indifferent aid workers, was a passing nightmare. The boyhood image he had of himself as a teacher and future village elder remained as real to him as it had ever been; he could not and would not give it up, just as he would not learn Egyptian Arabic, for to do so meant that he had accepted that he would never leave. And so he preferred not to seek out the company of the other Liberians, with similar pasts, young men like Abdula, who made jokes in an American accent learned from the tourists who used to come to Egypt before the specter of terrorism destroyed the holiday market, and who saw rebel soldiers burn his father over an open fire before hacking him into little pieces, or Mohamed, a tall boy with a moonlike face and frightened eyes, who watched as his godmother's head was kicked about like a football, or Abu, the boy soldier, whose rite of passage included the slitting open of a pregnant woman's stomach. What these lost boys had seen and been forced to do is not something others cared to hear about.

At the Mercy of the UNHCR

In Autumn, the early mornings in Cairo are almost cool. The pollution, which normally hangs over the streets like a heavy yellow blanket, is light and at this hour the city is still and quiet. Long before it is properly day, the asylum seekers gather at the gates of the offices of UNHCR. There are the Dinkas from Sudan with their very long legs, and the elegant high-cheekboned Somalis; some of the Sierra Leoneans have no arms or hands, the rebels there having decided that mutilating civilians was an effective way of terrorizing those who might be tempted to support the government. Then there are the Ethiopians, whose ancient allegiance to Haile Selassie has branded them as traitors to their country's new regime; men and women from Rwanda and Burundi, where massacres became a way of life; other Sudanese, dissident survivors of torture in Khartoum's security headquarters. They come at dawn to wait, in the hope that their names may feature on the new lists of those called for interview, to hand in documents, to jostle for a slip of paper with a date on which they can collect a form that will allow them to apply for an interview, many months, even years, into the future. Documents of any kind, even scraps of paper with a number on them, are infinitely precious: they suggest identity, a possible existence. Tattered high school certificates, old driver's licenses, envelopes with addresses on them, preserved against all odds during flight, are guarded and produced with pride. At UNHCR's gates all fear that they may learn that their appeal has failed and their file is closed, so that the future contains only statelessness or deportation. "Closed File," the terrible phrase that signifies the end of this particular road, is written in large black capital letters.

Since the middle of the 1980s, Egypt—along with forty other countries—has opted for the solution of having UN-HCR interview its asylum seekers in order to decide how well founded is their fear of persecution. The result is that the UN body, once revered for its mandate of protecting refugees, is, in Egypt, both prosecution and defense, an anomalous and uneasy position it occupies today with growing prickliness and suspicion. In 2000, 3,057 refugees left Cairo for new lives in the United States, Canada, and Australia (nearly all go to the United States). But after [the terrorist attacks of] September 11, 2001, President George W. Bush declined to fix a quota for that year's intake, thereby closing the door not only to the refugees who hoped to win places, but also to all those who had already been accepted but had not yet left and have now been told they need to be vetted again for possible terrorist links. No one really thinks that the United States will ever again be very welcoming to those persecuted in other lands.

Inside UNHCR's offices, where only those called for interview ever penetrate, there is an embattled air. It is not easy to be a gatekeeper to the future of so many desperate people; nor is it easy to keep in mind the intricacies of civil war and political repression across much of the African continent. Not all the young Egyptians employed to vet cases enjoy pronouncing on whether the violence suffered and remembered constitutes a degree of persecution extreme enough to make return too dangerous. In this daily listening for the nuances of deceit, the little lies that will mark a claim as false, something of UNHCR's noble mandate is being lost, but it is perhaps wrong to blame those who listen, hour after hour, to these tales of bloodshed and torture. There are too many cases, too much suffering, too little time. What is happening in Cairo today is happening all over the world; as the funds are cut and the number of asylum seekers keeps on growing, as the West becomes more fearful and more isolated, those who man the gates in Cairo are under pressure to search ever more keenly for lies and inconsistencies, while refugees despair.

A Former Chinese Political Prisoner Discusses His Detention

Luke Harding

In the following article Luke Harding interviews Wang Wanxing, who describes his life as a political dissident in China. The Universal Declaration of Human Rights guarantees all people the right to freely express their opinions, but Wang was sent to jail twice for his criticisms of the Chinese government. In 1992, three years after university students in Tiananmen Square were massacred for protesting against the government, Wang went to Tiananmen Square and held up a sign calling for greater human rights and democracy in China. This act landed him in the Ankang system of psychiatric hospitals that hold many of China's political prisoners. Most of the people held at Ankang hospitals are really mentally ill, but human rights activists believe that about three thousand political prisoners are held as well. Wang spent seven years at Ankang before he was released and expelled to Europe in 1999. Human Rights Watch and Amnesty International pressured the Chinese government to help bring about his release. Luke Harding works as a journalist for the Guardian. *He lives in London.*

It was as a small boy growing up in communist China that Wang Wanxing first had his doubts about the system. At school his teacher, Mr Li, extolled the virtues of Chairman [of the Communist Party from 1943–1976] Mao [Zedong]. Privately, however, Wang disliked Mao and disagreed with his criticism of [leader of the Soviet Union from 1953–1964 Ni-

Luke Harding, "G2: In the Grip of the Ankang: For 13 Years, Beijing Dissident Wang Wanxing Was Locked Up in a Brutal Psychiatric Hospital. Now Exiled to Germany, He Tells Luke Harding How China Is Using a Secret Network of Mental Institutions to Punish Political Prisoners," *The Guardian* (UK), December 20, 2005, p. 16. Copyright 2005 Guardian Newspapers Limited. Reproduced by permission of Guardian News Service, Ltd.

kita] Khrushchev. While he was at a middle school in Beijing, his antipathy grew when his grandmother starved to death in one of China's rural famines. It was from these early beginnings that Wang eventually became one of China's most famous dissidents—and shed rare light on one of the darkest aspects of the present regime: its systematic misuse of mental hospitals for political prisoners.

After a lifetime of dissent, Wang achieved international prominence in 1992 when he unfurled a banner in Tiananmen Square on the third anniversary of the 1989 student protests. The reaction was swift. He was arrested and dumped in a psychiatric hospital near Beijing, where he was to spend, apart from a short break, the next 13 years.

On August 16 [2005], the authorities released him and unexpectedly deported the 56-year-old Wang to Germany, where he was reunited with his wife and daughter, who had been living there as political refugees.

Wang's testimony is unique. He is the first high-profile dissident to be sent to Europe (rather than the US) since the late 80s, and the only inmate of China's notorious Ankang system of police-run psychiatric hospitals to be expelled to the west.

Wang's History of Protest

Sitting in his sixth-floor flat in Frankfurt, Wang—a spry figure who has recently taken up jogging—says he had never intended to become a dissident or political prisoner. His struggle against the Chinese authorities had happened pretty much by accident: "I don't really consider myself a hero. I think my conscience and intuition are not much different from other people's in China. My struggle came out of an attempt to help others."

Wang's parents—a labourer and an office worker—shared his doubts about Mao but said nothing. Wang was less circumspect. In 1968, with China gripped by the cultural revolution, the communist authorities sent him to a collective farm in Heilongjiang, a remote northern town next to China's river border with Russia. Here, he heaved rocks down from the mountains. "It was extremely hard work. There were young men and women there from across China. My pay was 32 yuan [£ 2.50] a month," Wang says.

While in exile, Wang began a one-man epistolary campaign against the might of the Chinese state, writing a personal letter to Mao urging him to reinstate the then disgraced Deng Xiaoping [de facto ruler of the People's Republic of China from 1976 to 1992] who had been the general secretary of the Communist party. The answer was swift: a week later three police cars turned up in the middle of the night and took him away. "I knew I was going to be arrested. But I also knew I was right," he says. He spent the next month in jail. When he got out his colleagues were unimpressed by his letter: "Most regarded me as stupid. All they could think about was getting back to Beijing."

In 1976, with mass popular demonstrations taking place in Tiananmen Square following the death of Zhou Enlai [premier of the People's Republic of China from 1949 to 1976], Wang wrote another letter, this time to China's premier Hua Guofeng, urging him to rehabilitate Deng Xiaoping. This time he was jailed for 17 months and branded a "reactionary". In February 1979, once Deng had returned to power, Wang was allowed to go back to Beijing, where he took a job in a vegetable warehouse. But his pro-democracy activities continued. In 1989 he met the student leaders at Beijing University who were organising the Tiananmen protests. Wang, however, did not agree with their methods. During a furious argument a group of students tipped him off his chair; others, he says, supported his belief that confrontation was wrong. "The massacres were very sad," he says.

Three years later, on June 4, 1992, Wang went back to Tiananmen Square and unfolded a banner calling for greater human rights and democracy. The police jumped on him and beat up journalists who captured his arrest on camera. "Many people grabbed me. I gave my banner to the police. I also gave them a cassette of a 24-page letter I'd written," Wang says. "They took me to the police station and took my photo. I spent three or four hours crouched on the floor, my head between my arms."

Wang Is Sent to Ankang

It was at this point that Wang was transferred into the Ankang system, a secret network of special psychiatric hospitals in which people who have committed no crime other than failing to agree with the government can be confined indefinitely without trial. As in the old Soviet Union, China classifies dissidents as being "mentally ill", arguing that their activities against the state are a form of madness. Human rights campaigners believe some 3,000 "political" inmates are currently kept in the hospitals [as of 2005], though the precise figure isn't known. The numbers have been swelled in recent years with the jailing of numerous practitioners belonging to the Falun Gong dissident movement, as well as local activists who have complained about corruption or poor working conditions. There are around 25 Ankang—the name means "peace and health"—institutes for the criminally insane in China; the government's eventual plan is to build one Ankang for every city with a population of one million or more.

After his arrest, meanwhile, Wang was "diagnosed" as suffering from "political monomania"—a condition that doesn't exist. Over cups of raspberry tea in his Frankfurt flat, and while his wife fries dumplings next door, Wang produces photographs of his hospital—prison—an old, brown-brick complex in Fangshan, some 70kms [43.75 miles] outside Beijing. One photo is particularly striking. It shows Wang in 1994 wearing striped prison clothes, in the hospital canteen. The canteen's peeling walls are a lurid turquoise; it looks as if Wang is drowning at the bottom of a terrible green sea.

The majority of inmates in the hospital really were mentally ill, Wang says, with he and one other political prisoner the only exceptions. "It was terrible. The hospital was terrible," he continues. "There were very many crazy people. The inmates would beat each other up. There was no safety.

"Two nurses at the hospital struggled to cope with up to 70 patients," he says; it was a regime of mismanagement and anarchy. The treatment meted out to inmates included electric shocks, insulin shocks and forced injections. "One prisoner, Huang Youliang, went on hunger strike. After he tore up his blanket the nurses let the other patients jump on him and force food down his throat. He choked. I watched him die. Another farmer, who was slightly wrong in the head, was given an electroshock during acupuncture treatment. He also died.

"The days were the same. We were woken at 6 A.M. and had breakfast at 7 A.M. There was a roll call. There was lunch, a nap and dinner. The rules were, don't run away, and don't kill anybody."

Wang avoided confrontation with hospital staff. At first the nurses forced him to take anti-psychotic drugs, which left him tired and dizzy; later the drugs stopped. (Often, he managed to hide the tablets in his mouth and spit them out.) Wang's fame abroad meant that he led a relatively privileged existence. He was allowed to listen to the BBC, and to have monthly visits from his wife, Wang Junying. "We got one hour only. Sometimes people were watching," Junying says.

Wang's Release

In 1999, seven years after he was first admitted, the authorities discharged him—under pressure from Human Rights Watch and Amnesty International. Three months later, however, he was readmitted. Wang had informed the hospital director that he intended to hold a press conference about his ordeal; she tipped off the Public Security Bureau (PSB) which runs the Ankang. He was rearrested.

The reasons for Wang's abrupt expulsion to Germany [in summer 2005] remain mysterious. Brad Adams, the executive director of Human Rights Watch in Asia, is not convinced Wang's release is part of a trend. "It's good news for Wang. But there is a whole warehouse full of people like him still kept in police-run mental hospitals," he says. "There is no real evidence that China is rethinking its policy of using psychiatry against dissidents."

Wang, however, believes he got out because of internal power struggles within the communist party, following the death of Deng Xiaoping and the loss of influence by Jiang Zemin, China's former president. During a four-hour interview at Wang's new home, he shows no sign of illness. He is alert, lucid and compelling. Ironically, his political demands are not even especially revolutionary. He merely wants a division of powers within China so that the government, army and communist party are separated. He would like rival political parties to exist. And having spent 13 years in it, he wants the Chinese government to reform the mental health system.

Since arriving in Frankfurt, he has spent time with his 25-year-old daughter Mai Xi, a student. He is thinking about writing his autobiography and learning German. His wife, who arrived in Germany in 2003, is still struggling with the language: helpful words and phrases are posted on the door. The flat echoes with her laughter as she tries to make herself understood. Will he ever go back to China? "Not at the moment. But I expect there will be changes in China by 2008. It might be possible then."

An Aid Worker Describes Working in Sudan During the Civil War

"Sleepless in Sudan"

The following selection is an excerpt from the "blog," or Web log, of an aid worker in Sudan who identifies herself as Sleepless in Sudan. Since 2003 Sudan has been embroiled in an ethnic conflict between the Sudanese Liberation Army (SLA), whose members are mostly from black African tribes, and the government of Sudan, which is controlled by Arabs. In 2003 a government-sponsored militia began to target and attack black African civilians in Darfur, a region in the north of Sudan. According to Human Rights Watch and Amnesty International, this government-sponsored ethnic cleansing in Darfur is a serious human rights violation. The Universal Declaration of Human Rights guarantees all people the right to security and freedom from torture and cruel treatment. In these three postings from early December 2005, Sleepless in Sudan describes problems with maintaining the safety of the roads in Sudan, the lack of supplies and money suffered by humanitarian aid workers, the lawlessness of Darfur, and her Sudanese friends' perception of the International Criminal Court.

Wednesday, December 14, 2005

Justice is big issue in a place like Darfur—basically, everyone agrees there is not enough of it. Not surprisingly, this means people are not particularly worried about being prosecuted when they continue to harass, abuse, rape or kill someone.

My Sudanese colleagues, especially those with a legal background, regularly try to rope me into long, passionate debates

"Sleepless in Sudan," www.sleeplessinsudan.blogspot.com, December 2005. Reproduced by permission.

about impunity, and ask me what I know about the progress of the International Criminal Court (the ICC, the organisation that has been tasked with investigating war crimes in Darfur).

I tell them about the updates that the ICC's chief prosecutor, Luis Moreno Ocampo, gives to the UN Security Council [the organ of the UN mandated with keeping international peace and security] . . . , and also about reports like the ones by Human Rights Watch (which [in December 2005] published a list of Sudanese officials who should be investigated for crimes against humanity in Darfur).

What always strikes me most about these conversations is not just the hope that people place in these international proceedings but more importantly the complete and utter distrust that they harbour towards their own government and its ability to bring any justice to Darfur.

It's not just that everyone instinctively mistrusts the government, which has made no secret of the fact that it hates the ICC (and which immediately organised protesters to march through the streets of Khartoum [the capital of Sudan] when the UN first asked the ICC to take on the case of Darfur in March 2005)—it also seems that none of my Sudanese friends has any illusions about the existence of an independent judiciary in Darfur.

"Those courts they have set up in Darfur, the ones that they want to use as a substitute for an ICC investigation, are pitiful," one of my friends scoffs when we read about new court rooms opening in Nyala and El Geneina in this week's papers. "They are just going to pick some random people from the streets and convict them for a handful of rapes and murders. They will do nothing for the victims of Darfur— they won't even scare any of the people who have committed the crimes. Anyway, many of them are now working for the police or the military themselves, there is no way these former

Janjaweed [the government-sponsored militia that in 2003 attacked civilian villages in Darfur] will turn on their own brothers and arrest them."

The ICC—unlike the local courts—does seem to scare people on the ground. "A lot of the Janjaweed leaders have gotten passports for themselves or members of their families, there are plenty who have already fled to Chad and Libya since March," colleagues in West Darfur claim.

"This is a real court, you can't buy yourself out of this one if they come after you. Even [the president of Sudan since 1993, Omar El] Bashir can't," one insists. Silently, I hope they are right.

Friday, December 09, 2005

An excellent article on IRIN [Integrated Regional Information Networks, a project of the UN Office for the Coordination of Humanitarian Affairs] gives a flavour of Darfur's current lawlessness (and the increased level of disgust that aid agency officials are publicly expressing about it): fresh clashes, attacks on towns and villages, destruction of desperately needed crops and wells, aid workers with guns pointed in their faces.

Finger-pointing has become almost meaningless in this context—no one with a gun is free from blame, whether it's the rebels, the government army, the police, or just random groups of thugs and bandits. The only consistency to the pattern is the fact that it's affecting all of Darfur—every single state has its own mess on its hands this month.

The violence has also been creeping from the countryside back into the towns. In El Geneina, the state capital of West Darfur, two NGO [non-governmental organization] guest houses have received night time visits from gun-toting bandits over the past 48 hours, and the fresh fighting around Um Gunya (an SLA stronghold just south of Nyala) could be heard loud and clear even in Kalma camp [a refugee camp in southern Darfur where the aid worker is stationed].

Despite the fact that the peace talks in Abuja [Nigeria's capital] have not yet collapsed, there's a new sense of doom and gloom on the ground. Pessimism and despair are the order of the day—no one inside the camps thinks they will be going home anytime soon, and the frustration is palpable.

I'm glad to see that *The Economist* [a British current events magazine] has published a front page article on Sudan this week, since this somehow always makes people in government offices sit up and take notice. Hopefully, they'll be taking the advice that the article gives—which includes more support to the African Union to keep the peace, and generally "kicking up more of a fuss" politically. Wise words.

Wednesday, December 07, 2005

Miraculously, there's some more good news from Kalma camp this week—the ban on 'commercial traffic' between the camp and Nyala town (which lies around 15km [9.3 miles] to the North-West of Kalma) is about to be lifted.

The aid agencies who work inside Kalma camp have been struggling to get this result for months—since the governor of South Darfur first instituted the ban seven months ago, it has created a lot of problems for the people of Kalma camp.

Essentially, the ban has been trapping the displaced families inside the camp—since it often prevented not just vehicles but even horse or donkey carts from moving back and forth between the camp and the town, people had very little chance to earn a living or set up little shops or markets inside the camp. Prices for basic goods—like clothes, vegetables or soap—immediately increased to amounts that were beyond the reach of many of the mothers I've met in Kalma.

For the 100,000+ people piled on top of each other on a few square kilometers of desert sand, this has been a frustrating and intensely debilitating situation (and it's not as if things in Darfur weren't bad enough already to start off with).

It seems that—after more than 200 days—the local authorities will finally be lifting the commercial ban on December 15th. Together with the recently revived firewood patrols around the camp, this small step will hopefully help to make life just a little bit easier for the people of Kalma. It's been long overdue. . . .

Sunday, December 04, 2005

The African Union (AU) is sending a team to Darfur to assess their lack of cash and equipment—finally. For months, AU officials have been trying to speak up about the woefully inadequate support they are getting from the international community.

"If you are supposed to move people with 20 vehicles and you are moving them with six vehicles, you can understand the problems," Festus Okonkwo, the military head of the AU mission, told Reuters today.

On the ground, I've heard a lot worse. There is no fuel for AU cars, never mind helicopters. Ammunition runs out (as it did during the attack that killed four Nigerian peacekeepers and two AU contractors in October). Soldiers routinely show up at aid agency compounds to ask if they can have some mosquito nets or even blankets. Civilian police officers walk around the camps unable to communicate with people because they have not yet sent them any translators. It's clear the AU has not been able to do its job—and there is still no one actually protecting those who need it most.

The AU has been remarkably transparent about many of these shortcomings—and clearly outlined challenges like the ones I've just talked about in their assessment report in March [2005].

Unfortunately, they still aren't getting the support and the cash they need. The US congress recently cut back on $50 million of funding they'd already pledged to the AU, and here in Khartoum everyone seems to be more interested in talking about how and when the UN can take over from the AU rather than discussing what could be done to help the troops who are already there.

In the meantime, the people in the camps are not getting any safer. If the last AU assessment is anything to go by, the forthcoming report on the state of the AU mission could well be a very useful and self-critical piece of work. My worry is that—as with the last one, when the team recommended a troop increase to 12,000 soldiers—no one will pay very much attention to it.

Saturday, December 03, 2005

I'm catching up on my work emails today, and a quick glance through the security reports confirms that West Darfur remains in a state of near anarchy. Most aid agencies stopped using the roads in this part of Darfur in August/September [2005], following daily attacks on humanitarian convoys. The situation had reached a level where you could pretty much be guaranteed to find yourself in an ambush if you used certain roads. Not surprisingly, many aid agencies have suspended their operations in certain areas, while others began to rely on UN helicopters to get around.

The two helicopters that are based in the El Geneina, the state capital, only have enough fuel for a certain amount of flights though (80 hrs per month I think—apparently there's no money in the UN coffers for more than that).

So now it seems that someone at the UN thought it would be a good idea to check if the roads have become a bit safer again—this helicopter business, after all, is becoming a pretty heavy drain on the budget.

"The UN road assessment of the Geneina-Mournei was conducted last week," I read in the security minutes. So far, so good.

(Before I go on, I will come out and ashamedly admit that I often find security procedures, meetings and reports over here in Darfur amusing. I know I shouldn't—this is serious stuff after all. But sometimes the information and reports are just so confusing and absurd that I can't help but laugh. In my defense, I think it's a relatively normal coping mechanism. All of us are doing it: for weeks, I have been engaged in an email battle with several colleagues to try and find more and more bizzare or funny security reports.)

So, back to minutes: "The UN road assessment of the Geneina-Mournei road was conducted last week."

Seems like a good idea, I think. Until I realise how the security assessment was actually carried out.

"Two UN vehicles with national and international staff were sent to check the safety of the road. [On] Habillah Konari road, the convoy was ambushed. Fortunately, the 2 cars were keeping space between each other and so the second car managed to escape and report the incident to the nearest police station. The ambushed car then joined the other one at the police station after the attackers had taken all the personal belongings of the staff in that car."

"Police responded straight away and the UN staff on their way back heard the shooting. As a result of this incident UN had suspended all the planned road assessment."

Now I'm not a security expert. I don't know how road assessments and security checks are usually carried out, or what would be the best way of going about them.

And it may just be me, but somehow, sending a few carloads full of staff into the danger zone to wait and see whether or not the bandits are still ambushing cars does not seem particularly sophisticated—or safe.

There are too many emails in my inbox to ponder security issues too long, so I just shrug and make a mental note to myself, "Geneina-Mournei road still not safe". I'm glad the UN is trying to check up on the security situation—someone needs to, because Darfur's still a mess. But today, I thank my lucky stars I am not working for a UN security assessment team.

The Former High Commissioner for Human Rights Discusses Key Human Rights Concerns

Mary Robinson, interviewed by Ian Williams

The following selection is the transcript of an interview with Mary Robinson, who served as the United Nations High Commissioner for Human Rights from 1997 to 2002. She gave this interview in 2002 as she was preparing to leave her post. She discusses her views on some of the key issues she dealt with during her five-year term. For example, she talks about how the Israeli occupation of Palestine has caused human rights abuses. She also explains how she has contributed to shifts in the international human rights agenda. For example, she remembers learning that people in some developing countries think that the human rights agenda is just another means of Western political domination. Robinson explains that policy makers such as herself have responded to this criticism by focusing more on economic and social development as part of their policies. She also discusses how the terrorist attacks of September 11, 2001, have affected the human rights agenda, the controversial role of the World Trade Organization in international development, and the changing approach to human rights in an increasingly Westernized China. Mary Robinson is interviewed by Ian Williams, who is the United Nations correspondent for the Nation.

Robinson became the second United Nations high commissioner for human rights in June 1997 after resigning as president of Ireland. Before Robinson, Ireland's presidency was a ceremonial office, whose holder was expected to do little

Mary Robinson, interviewed by Ian Williams, "Mary Robinson Interview," Salon.com, July 26, 2002. This article first appeared in Salon.com, at http://www.salon.com. An online version remains in the Salon archives. Reproduced with permission.

more than shake hands with VIPs and open schools and hospitals. But when Robinson—a woman with socialist and feminist leanings—was elected, it symbolized the changes in what had been a traditionally conservative and religion-dominated country. She stretched the boundaries of the presidency to fit her concerns, one of the most prominent of which was human rights. She made trips to places like Somalia and Rwanda, and in the Great Lakes region of Africa she coined the memorable phrase, "the cycle of impunity," to describe the process by which leaving mass murder unpunished encouraged others to do the same.

Her name had actually been raised as a replacement for Boutros Boutros Ghali at the head of the U.N., but although she was the right gender, Ireland was not in Africa, and that was where the consensus said that the next secretary general should come from. And when he did, Kofi Annan tapped her for the human rights job. As high commissioner for human rights, she brought a sense of urgency to the position, and the authority of a recently retired head of state. It irked the type of U.N. bureaucrats who would much rather file reports of massacres at the bottom of a cabinet than upset governments. For her, human rights transcended national affiliations. For example, just because China was big, or Israel had friends in Washington, was no reason to stay silent.

The word went around in the corridors of power in Washington and New York's U.N. headquarters. She was "difficult to work with." Just because the U.S. and Israel walked out of the Durban Conference [a UN world conference against racism held in Durban, South Africa, in 2001], she saw no reason to close it down when the rest of the world stayed. She was forthright about abuses of human rights by both Israel and the Palestinian Authority: In Washington she was damned.

However, though she leaves the U.N. in a matter of weeks, Robinson refuses to limp like a lame duck. Recently, she was in New York to report to the Security Council on the massacres and the human rights situation in the Congo and was as forthright as ever before giving up what she calls "the day job."

Williams: Putting it politely, from the outside it looks as if the Middle East issue was the one that led to, shall we say, diminished enthusiasm for your renewal in office. Is that a fair assessment?

Robinson: Indeed. It's ironic in a way, because the issue I'm most committed to is the integrity of the human rights agenda, and shaping it so it's not politicized. I applied that faithfully to addressing the problems both in the occupied Palestinian Territory and in Israel, and I have mentally, emotionally and intellectually tried to be bound by it. I may have made some mistakes but that is where I'm at, because that is essentially the core of why I took this job.

It was very interesting to me that it is not so perceived on the Israeli side. It may be because I've been over-appreciated on the Palestinian side. But I have condemned unequivocally suicide bombing, and reiterated the need for human security in Israel for political debate.

Even then, in 2000, it was very evident that the occupation is at the root of many of the human rights problems, and the intifada, which had started then, was only at the stage of stone throwing and young people being killed. Since then we have drive-by shootings and suicide bombing which is of course appalling and cannot be condemned strongly enough, certainly not justified by any cause—but the Israeli responses are also excessive.

It worries me that in this great country [the U.S.] that's not the perception: They don't see the suffering of the Palestinian people; they don't see the impact of collective punishment. They do immediately see and empathize—and rightly—with the suffering of Israeli civilians who are killed, or injured, or just frightened, and of course I do too. But I find it very disheartening that there is not more understanding here of the appalling suffering of the Palestinian population, nor appreciation that this is not going to lead to a secure future. It's going to lead to greater hatred and desperation, of further suicide bombings. . . .

Now, after five years as high commissioner, do you think you have made a difference?

Certainly there's been a change . . . I [recently] addressed the Security Council [organ of the UN responsible for maintaining international peace and security] on the Democratic Republic of the Congo and they will publish my report as a document. Five years ago, the S.C. [Security Council] would not have listened to a high commissioner!

There's also been a dramatic shift, and one that I do take some credit for, in the developing world's attitude. When I started back in September of 1997, I was quite taken aback by how many leaders of developing countries told me: "Don't you know human rights is just a Western stick to beat us with? It is politicized, nothing to do with real concern about human rights."

You know, there was an element of truth in that, and so I found it necessary to find, first of all, the true agenda of human rights at the international level. That is to be strong in civil liberties, in the protection and promotion of civil and political rights, and strong in the protection and promotion of economic, social and cultural rights, and to fulfill the express vision and mandate of the establishment of the high commissioner's office, which was to seek consensus on the right to development. That's an individual and a collective right, the right of the people to gain the full flower of their human rights.

And that led to more linkage being made by leaders of developing countries between human rights and economic and social development. They began to realize that if you got your human rights right, you accelerated human development, economic development ... What is very clear is that human rights need protection at national and local level, and therefore unless there is more attention to strengthening human rights, and law and administration of justice at national level, then we are not really going to make great progress.

It's reflected very dramatically in the New Economic Partnership for African Development, the NEPAD. The text of that is an extraordinary indication of how far human rights have moved to become the priority tool of developing countries in making progress. They identified the four priority areas: to strengthen the administration of justice, the rule of law, tackling corruption, and adhering fully to international human rights norms and standards ... To me it is a moral as well as a practical issue. If countries give priority to these issues and cannot find the resources domestically—then that's certainly an area I'm going to address by trying to build quiet alliances for it for when I quit the day job. . . .

Your concerns have not always been shared by some international organizations: the World Bank and IMF [International Monetary Fund] traditionally never let a few prison camps interfere with their appreciation of a good GDP [gross domestic product, a measure of economic strength] growth rate. Have you turned them round yet?

Certainly, our office is working, particularly with the World Bank [W.B.] but also the IMF and WTO [World Trade Organization], and we're engaged in a very significant analysis of poverty reduction strategies and we're developing human rights guidelines for them, with close involvement of the W.B., the IMF, and the WTO. This would not have happened two years ago. It's a really interesting intellectual development. Human rights lawyers are listening to economists and vice versa in seeing how the human rights norms and standards can be a positive framework for addressing poverty, because they address participation; it gives civil society tools to measure whether there is progressive implementation of the right to education, right to health, to food, without discrimination against minorities, indigenous people.

The World Trade Organization especially has been seen as totally heartless and ethics-free by design. Have you really given them a heart transplant?

It's true that trade ministers going into the WTO meetings don't bring with them, as I believe they should, a consciousness of the commitments their governments have made to ratify covenants and conventions. Equally, we don't have a situation that it's in the front of the mind of the IMF. In a country like Argentina, where there are problems, is there sufficient consciousness to help such a government that has ratified the Covenant on Economic, Cultural and Social Rights, or the Convention on the Rights of the Child to carry through on that, and to progressively implement these rights, or is the emphasis all on structural adjustment? So we need "joined up" government that brings the human rights commitment into the WTO.

At the moment, many governments all over the world are joining up to throw human rights overboard as part of the struggle against terrorism using Sept. 11 as an excuse. If you think you'd made progress before, don't you see lots of it evaporating?

It's a very serious concern. I was struck last month when we had the annual meeting of the rapporteurs and the coming together of the chairs of the treaty bodies, that all these experts were concerned about the deteriorating situation after Sept. 11. We all recognize the importance of human security, of coalitions against terrorism, of Security Council Resolution 1473 [calling for joint action against terrorism], but nonetheless the impact on the ground is very worrying for human rights. Governments are using it to clamp down on human rights and freedom of expression—human rights defenders branded as terrorists; the harsh climate for asylum seekers and refugees. The worrying thing is that secure democracies such as the U.S. are not holding the standards properly. Just look at the treatment of prisoners in Guantánamo Bay, and even more so those who have been arrested under immigration laws with no access to lawyers and no information. Nobody knows exactly what his or her situation is.

You have worked hard to engage China, and you were attacked by some of the Irish press for pandering to the occupiers of Tibet. How successful has your engagement with the Chinese been?

In fact, I was impressed by how far we've been able to come since that first visit [to China] in September 1998. When I go back in August for a workshop on the independence of lawyers and judges, it will be my sixth visit as high commissioner. We've had an intensive series of workshops with them, on re-education through labor, on the police and human rights, devising a human rights training manual for the police, on human rights education and to insert human rights values in the [school] curriculum on secondary and tertiary levels.

But I have no illusions. None of this means we have changed things overnight. On the other hand, nor does a technical cooperation program mean that I don't speak out on human rights issues. Every time I've been in China, I've been very tough on how they treat the Falun Gong [a religious sect labeled a seditious cult by the Chinese government], on their treatment of political dissidents. When I went in November [2001] after Sept. 11, I made the point to them that they were using it to be more severe on the Uighur population [a Muslim community], branding them as terrorists in a way that had not been done before.

So I take up all these issues: They do say to me now, "We know your habits." But that being said, I'm impressed with the progress we've made. When the Chinese sign a covenant, they do it for Chinese reasons—and they are quite serious about it.

So we shouldn't underestimate what can be done. Even some of the federations, like the All China Federation of Women, are becoming more and more independent and more and more concerned with the rights of women.

Also, the last time I was there they were taking courageous stands as women in their own area to bring home that the denial and stigma attached to HIV/AIDS meant that there would be a rampant HIV/AIDS problem.

One phrase you coined that will surely live on is "the cycle of impunity." You used it in Central Africa to describe how each person who committed genocide thought they could get away with it because their predecessors had. Has the International Criminal Court [ICC] put the brake on the cycle, or is it just symbolic?

I really think the ICC is an extraordinary step forward, a very important institution, a way of symbolizing that we are going to end impunity for egregious human rights violations. It may take time, but now there is going to be a permanent court, and you can be brought before it if you haven't been before a national court.

I really regret, first of all, the "unsigning" of the statute by the United States. You know, we deal with the integrity and strength of what we build up in human rights, and part of it is that when we sign and ratify instruments we stand by them. What the U.S. has done is to create uncertainty. Signing is usually an indication that ratification is on the way. Now if other countries are under pressure on human rights instruments they've signed, they may say "Well, the U.S. can unsign a treaty, then so can we."

Secondly, I found the controversy about peacekeepers to be very sad. The political resolution of it has angered the human rights community, but it's more important that we get back to strengthening the court. There have been 76 ratifications. Mexico and others are on the way. There will soon be 100 or more.

Organizations to Contact

American Civil Liberties Union (ACLU)
132 W. 43rd St., New York, NY 10036
(212) 944-9800 • fax: (212) 869-9065
e-mail: aclu@aclu.org
Web site: www.aclu.org

The ACLU is a national organization that works to defend Americans' civil rights as guaranteed by the U.S. Constitution. The ACLU strives to assure equality before the law regardless of race, color, sexual orientation or national origin. This organization publishes and distributes policy statements and pamphlets on topics such as the death penalty. The ACLU also publishes the semiannual newsletter *Civil Liberties Alert* and the annual *International Civil Liberties Report*.

Amnesty International (AI)
322 8th Ave., New York, NY 10001
(212) 807-8400 • fax: (212) 473-9193
e-mail: admin-us@aiusa.org
Web site: www.amnestyusa.org

Amnesty International is a worldwide, independent volunteer movement that works to promote internationally recognized human rights. It also aims to free people detained for their beliefs but who have not used or advocated violence, as well as people imprisoned because of their ethnic origin, gender, language, national or social origin, economic status, or country of birth. AI seeks to ensure fair and prompt trials for political prisoners and to abolish torture, "disappearances," cruel treatment of prisoners, and executions. Its publications include a quarterly newsletter, *Amnesty Action*; an annual book, *Amnesty International Report*; and papers and special reports on a wide variety of human rights issues, such as the death penalty, women's issues, and refugees.

The Carr Center for Human Rights Policy
John F. Kennedy School of Government
Cambridge, MA 02138
(617) 495-5819 • fax: (617) 495-4297
e-mail: carr_center@ksg.harvard.edu
Web site: www.ksg.harvard.edu/cchrp/index.shtml

The Carr Center for Human Rights Policy is a research and education institution that trains future human rights leaders and seeks to lead public policy debate on human rights. It also partners with human rights organizations to help them respond to current and future human rights challenges.

The Carter Center
One Copenhill, 453 Freedom Pkwy., Atlanta, GA 30307
(404) 420-5100
e-mail: carterweb@emory.edu
Web site: www.cartercenter.org/default.asp

The Carter Center is a nongovernmental organization in partnership with Emory University and is dedicated to improving human rights through development projects and advocacy. The Carter Center's development projects include the dissemination of agricultural techniques to increase food production in Sub-Saharan Africa and a global mental health program, which seeks to improve services and treatment for those who suffer from mental illnesses. The Carter Center also advocates for human rights around the globe. The publications of the Carter Center include the monthly newsletter *News and Views from the Carter Center.*

Center for Constitutional Rights
666 Broadway, 7th Floor, New York, NY 10012
(212) 614-6464 • fax: (212) 614-6499
e-mail: info@ccr_ny.org
Web site: www.ccr_g90ny.org/v2/home.asp

The Center for Constitutional Rights is a nonprofit organization committed to protecting and advancing the rights guaranteed by the U.S. Constitution and the Universal Declaration of Human Rights. The Center uses education and litigation to empower poor communities and communities of color, to protect the rights of those with the least access to legal resources, and to train attorneys in constitutional and human rights. They publish various pamphlets and fact sheets including *Pioneering the Field of Civil Human Rights Law* and *Against War with Iraq: An Anti-war Primer.*

Human Rights Watch

350 Fifth Ave., 34th Floor, New York, NY 10118-3299
(212) 290-4700 • fax: (212) 736-1300
e-mail: hrwny@hrw.org
Web site: www.hrw.org

Human Rights Watch investigates human rights abuses in more than seventy countries around the world. It promotes civil liberties and defends freedom of thought, due process, and equal protection under the law. Its goal is to hold governments accountable for human rights violations. It publishes the annual *Human Rights Watch World Report.*

International Organization for Migration (IOM)

17, Route des Morillons, Geneva 19 CH-1211
    Switzerland
+41 22 717 9111 • fax: +41 22 798 6150
e-mail: info@iom.int
Web site: www.iom.int

The International Organization for Migration (IOM) works with migrants and governments to make sure that the human rights of migrants are respected. Their projects include countering human trafficking, rapid humanitarian responses to sudden migration flows, and assistance to migrants on their way to new homes and lives. Among the IOM's publications are the newsletter *Migration* and the *International Dialogue on Migration.*

Minority Rights Group International (MRG)

54 Commercial St., London E1 6LT
   UK
+44 (0)20 7422 4200 • fax: +44 (0)20 7422 4201
e-mail: minority.rights@mrgmail.org
Web site: www.minorityrights.org

Minority Rights Group International advocates for the rights of ethnic, religious, and linguistic minorities and indigenous peoples worldwide. MRG is a nonpartisan, nongovernmental organization that lobbies decision makers and campaigns in communities to convince them of the need for long-term, sustainable improvement of minority group rights. MRG also raises awareness of the situation of minorities and indigenous peoples among the general public. MRG publishes several reports, training manuals, and policy reports that are available on their Web site.

New York Immigration Coalition

275 7th Ave., 9th Floor, New York, NY 10001
(212) 627-2227 • fax: (212) 627-9314
Web site: www.thenyic.org/index.asp

The New York Immigration Coalition is an education and advocacy group that serves as an umbrella organization for approximately 150 groups in New York State that work with immigrants and refugees. Their activities include fighting for the reform of U.S. immigration policy, voter registration and education, and workshops and community education events on immigration and social services law. They publish the monthly newsletter *NYIC Immigration News* and many reports including *Denied at the Door: Language Barriers Block Immigrant Parents from School Involvement*.

Save the Children

54 Wilton Rd., Westport, CT 06880
(203) 221-4030
Web site: www.savethechildren.org/index.asp

Save the Children is an international relief and development organization dedicated to creating lasting change for children in need around the world. Their many publications include *Protecting Children in Emergencies: Escalating Threats to Children Must Be Addressed.* They also publish annual reports and an e-newsletter.

United Nations

UN Headquarters, First Ave. at 46th St., New York, NY 10017

Web site: www.un.org/english

The United Nations Secretariat and UN programs, such as the UN Children's Fund (UNICEF) and the UN Development Program (UNDP), provide technical assistance and other forms of practical help in virtually all areas of economic and social endeavor including the protection of Human Rights. The United Nations publishes many books and documents on human rights, including *Economic, Social and Cultural Rights: Handbook for National Human Rights Institutions* and *The Globalization of Human Rights.*

Bibliography

Books

Timothy C. Brown — *The Real Contra War: Highlander Peasant Resistance in Nicaragua.* Norman: University of Oklahoma Press, 2001.

Ken Conca — *Governing Water: Contentious Transnational Politics and Global Institution Building.* Cambridge, MA: MIT Press, 2006.

Romeo Dallaire — *Shake Hands with the Devil: the Failure of Humanity in Rwanda.* Toronto: Random House Canada, 2003.

Janet Dine — *Companies, International Trade and Human Rights.* New York: Cambridge University Press, 2005.

Mark Ensalaco and Linda C. Majka — *Children's Human Rights: Progress and Challenges for Children Worldwide.* Lanham, MD: Rowman & Littlefield, 2005.

Paul Farmer — *Pathologies of Power: Health, Human Rights and the New War on the Poor.* Berkeley: University of California Press, 2003.

Ann Fagan Ginger — *Challenging U.S. Human Rights Violations Since 9/11.* Amherst, MA: Prometheus, 2005.

Merle Goldman — *From Comrade to Citizen: Struggle for Political Rights in China.* Cambridge, MA: Harvard University Press, 2005.

Ana Gonzalez-Paez — *Human Rights and World Trade: Hunger in International Society.* New York: Routledge, 2005.

Michael Goodhart — *Democracy as Human Rights: Freedom and Equality in the Age of Globalization.* New York: Routledge, 2005.

Sofia Gruskin et al. — *Perspectives on Health and Human Rights.* New York: Routledge, 2005.

Tajeldin I. Hamad, Frederick A. Swarts, and Anne Ranniste Smart — *Culture of Responsibility and the Role of NGOs.* St. Paul, MN: Paragon House, 2003.

Thom Hartman — *Unequal Protection: The Rise of Corporate Dominance and the Theft of Human Rights.* New York: St. Martin's, 2002.

Shireen T. Hunter and Huma Malik — *Islam and Human Rights: Advancing a U.S.-Muslim Dialogue.* Washington, DC: Center for Strategic and International Studies, 2005.

Michael Ignatieff — *American Exceptionalism and Human Rights.* Princeton, NJ: Princeton University Press, 2005.

Virginia A. Leary and Daniel Warner — *Social Issues, Globalization and International Institutions: Labour Rights and the EU, ILO, OECD and WTO.* Boston: M. Nijhoff, 2006.

Beatriz Manz   *Paradise in Ashes: A Guatemalan Journey of Courage, Terror and Hope.* Berkeley: University of California Press, 2004.

Sally Engle Merry   *Human Rights and Gender Violence: Translating International Law into Local Justice.* Chicago: University of Chicago Press, 2006.

Obioma Nnaemeka and Joy Ngozi Ezeilo   *Engendering Human Rights: Cultural and Socioeconomic Realities in Africa.* New York: Palgrave Macmillan, 2005.

Bahram Ghazi Shariat Panahi   *IMF, the World Bank Group, and the Question of Human Rights.* New York: Transnational, 2005.

David Rieff   *At the Point of a Gun: Democratic Dreams and Armed Intervention.* New York: Simon & Schuster, 2005.

Margot E. Salomon   *Economic, Social and Cultural Rights: A Guide for Minorities and Indigenous Peoples.* London: Minority Rights Group International, 2005.

Horacio Verbitsky   *Confessions of an Argentine Dirty Warrior: A Firsthand Account of Atrocity.* New York: New Press, 2005.

Burns H. Weston   *Child Labor and Human Rights: Making Children Matter.* Boulder, CO: Lynne Rienner, 2005.

Richard Ashby Wilson   *Human Rights in the War on Terror.* New York: Cambridge University Press, 2005.

Alicia Ely Yamin   *Learning to Dance: Advancing Women's Reproductive Health and Well-Being from the Perspective of Public Health and Human Rights.* Cambridge, MA: Harvard University Press, 2005.

Periodicals

Denis Arnold and Laura Hartman   "Beyond Sweatshops: Positive Deviancy and Global Labor Practices," *Business Ethics*, July 2005.

Moustafa Bavoumi   "Disco Inferno," *Nation*, December 26, 2005.

Jo Becker   "Child Soldiers: Changing a Culture of Violence," *Human Rights*, Winter 2005.

Elaine Chang   "Stolen Childhoods," *Ecologist*, November/December 2005.

Jonathan Cohen, Rebecca Schleifer, and Tony Tate   "AIDS in Uganda: The Human Rights Dimension," *Lancet*, June 18–24, 2005.

Ariel Colonomos and Javier Santiso   "Vive la France! French Multinationals and Human Rights," *Human Rights Quarterly*, November 2005.

Mark Dowie   "Conservation Refugees: When Protecting Nature Means Kicking People Out," *Orion*, November/December 2005.

Daniel Drezner and Henry Farrell   "Web of Influence," *Foreign Policy*, November/December 2004.

Economist	"It'll Do What It Can Get Away With—Sudan," December 3 2005.
Dorinda Elliot	"The Last Frontier," *Time*, June 27, 2005.
Nancy Gallagher	"Amnesty International and the Idea of Muslim Women's Human Rights," *Journal of Middle East Women's Studies*, Fall 2005.
Kurt Henne and David Moseley	"Combating the Worst Forms of Child Labor in Bolivia," *Human Rights*, Winter 2005.
Elizabeth Kuznesof	"The House, the Street, Global Society: Latin American Families and Childhood," *Journal of Social History*, Summer 2005.
David Moberg	"Human Rights at Work," *Nation*, December 26, 2005.
Eric Neurmayer	"Do International Human Rights Treaties Improve Respect for Human Rights?" *Journal of Conflict Resolution*, December 2005.
New American	"The Bloody Border," June 13, 2005.
New Republic	"Open Secrets," May 17, 2004.
Anjula Razdan	"Hosed: Big Water Is Starting to Look Like Big Oil," *Utne*, November/December 2005.
Layla M. Shaaban and Sarah Harbison	"Reaching the Tipping Point Against Female Genital Mutilation," *Lancet*, July 30–August 5, 2005.

Andre Stemmett "International Law and the Use of Force: Some Post 9/11 Perspectives," *Rusi Journal*, October 2003.

Evan Thomas and Michael Hirsh "The Debate over Torture: Right After 9/11 Cheney Said, 'We Have to Work . . . the Dark Side If You Will,'" *Newsweek*, November 21, 2005.

Richard A. Webster "Orleans Parish Prison Inmates Say They Were Mistreated as Katrina's Floodwaters Rose," *New Orleans City-Business*, January 23, 2006.

Stacey Williams "One Strike, You're Out," *Chicago Reporter*, July/August 2005.

Kenji Yoshino "The Pressure to Cover," *New York Times Magazine*, January 15, 2006.

Index

Abu Ghraib prison, 89
  Arab view of democracy and, 50
Adams, Brad, 137
Al-Affendiand, 42
African Commission on Human and Peoples' Rights, 61
African Union (AU), 61
  Darfur mission of, 59, 141
  lack of support for, 142–43
Ahmed, Mohammad Aziz, 41, 42, 43
Alien Tort Claims Act (1789), 99
All China Federation of Women, 152
amnesty, for gross violators of human rights, 34
Amnesty International, 12, 52, 89
  on Bush administration's human rights record, 89
  UN human rights work and, 109, 136
Annan, Kofi, 102–103, 146
  on mission of United Nations, 107
  on opening of 2005 session of Commission on Human Rights, 110
  on UN state-building initiatives, 108
Ashcroft, John, 99
asylum
  right to, in Universal Declaration of Human Rights, 21
  see also refugees
authoritarianism, 40
  human rights in nations with histories of, 84
Axworthy, Lloyd, 114
Al-Azhar, 42

El-Bashir, Omar, 66, 140
Beijing Fourth World Conference on Women, 119
bin Laden, Osama, 50
Boggs, Catherine, 100
Brazil, 80
  minority rights in, 83
Buergenthal, Thomas, 30
Building Democratic Institutions (Cheema), 77
Burma. See Myanmar
Bush, George W., 12, 85
  on trade and spread of democracy, 90
Bush administration
  opposition of, to lawsuits against corporations, 99
  relations between Uzbekistan and, 48
  views of, on Guantánamo detainees, 69
Bush doctrine, contradictions in, 49–51

"Cairo Declaration of Human Rights, The" (Organization of the Islamic Conference), 42, 44
Cassin, René, 104
Cato Institute, 90, 93
Center for Constitutional Rights, 73
Cheema, G. Shabbir, 77
Cheney, Dick, 69
China, People's Republic of
  Ankang system in, 132, 135–36
  economic reform in, 93–94
    liberal reform vs., 14
  human rights in constitution of, 52

human rights violations by
  against religious/spiritual groups, 55–56
  against Uighurs, 57–58
  against women, 54–55
influence of, on world trade, 14
Internet restrictions in, 87
political targets of, 53
protests in, 54
UN achievements in, 151–52
CHR. *See* United Nations Human Rights Commission
civil wars, minority rights during, 84
CNN.com, 85
Cold War, 28, 39
  human rights and end of, 32
Colombia, 88
Commission on Human Rights (CHR), on Darfur, 65
Convention Relating to the Status of Refugees, 124–25
corporations, multinational
  cases charging complicity with repressive governments by, 97–98
  human rights and power of, 12
  local response to overseas conduct of, 100
  pressure on, to increase oil production, 101
Council of Europe, 36
Cuba, 88
cultural relativism, Islamic human rights and, 42
cultural rights, in Universal Declaration of Human Rights, 24

Darfur Commission Report, 64
Darfur (Sudan), 62–63
  attacks on aid workers in, 143–44
  beginning of crisis in, 63–64
  death toll in, 64–65
  ethnic cleansing in, 59
  issue of justice in, 138–40
  Kalma camp, 141–42
death penalty, in China, 56
Declaration of Independence, 31
Declaration of the Rights of Man and of the Citizen, 31
Declaration on the Rights of Persons Belonging to National or Ethnic, Religious and Linguistic Minorities, 36
democracies
  economic and social rights in, 81–82
  income disparities in, 80
  minority rights in, 82–84
democracy
  Bush doctrine and, 48–51
  defining features of, 78–80
  globalization and spread of, 92–94
  historic separation between human rights and, 77–78
  Internet as tool of, 117–19
Deng Xiaoping, 134, 137
Ding Zilin, 53
Doha Development Round, 94–95
Dostum, Abdul Rashid, 72
"Draft Islamic Constitution" (Al-Azhar), 42
Durban Conference (2001), 146

Economic and Social Council (ECOSOC), 108–109
Economist (magazine), 13, 14, 141
education
  of police officers/soldiers, 27
  right to, in Universal Declaration of Human Rights, 12, 23–24
Egeland, Jan, 65
Egypt, 87

elections
>in Afghanistan and Iraq, 87
>Bush doctrine and, 50, 51
>as essential feature of democracies, 78
>influence of the wealthy on, 81
>Serbian, Internet use and, 119
>in Universal Declaration of Human Rights, 22
>UN monitoring of, 107–108
>in Uzbekistan, 48

El Geneina (West Darfur), 140, 143

equal protection of law, in Universal Declaration of Human Rights, 19

Erdogan, Recep Tayyip, 13

ethnic cleansing
>in Darfur, 63–65
>in former Yugoslavia, 36

European Convention on Human Rights, 37

Eviatar, Daphne, 96

Falun Gong, 53, 55, 135–36, 151

Fontaine, Phil, 114

For the Record: the UN Human Rights System (Human Rights Internet), 120

Framework Convention for the Protection of National Minorities (Council of Europe), 36

Freedom House, 92

Freeland, Jonathan, 47

G8, 115

Geneva Conventions, 32

Al-Ghanoushi, 42

Ghitis, Frida, 111

Global Information Network, 12–13

globalization
>Muslim responses to, 41
>spread of democracy and, 92–94

Green, Jennie, 98

Griswold, Daniel, 90

Guantánamo Bay prison camp, 67, 68, 89
>detainees at, 151
>>children as, 75
>>innocents victims among, 71–72, 74
>>lack of information about, 68–69
>tribunals at, 69–70
>Uighurs held at, 58

Guofeng, Hua, 134

Habermas, Jürgen, 103, 109

Habib, Mamdouh, 74

Harding, Luke, 132

Hariri, Rafiq, 88

Harrell-Bond, Barbara, 124

Hitler, Adolf, 36

Huang Youliang, 136

humanitarian military intervention (HMI), Darfur crisis and debate on right to, 61

human rights
>Cold War and, 32
>corporate interests vs., 12
>economic development and, 28
>growing attention to, 39–40
>historic separation between democracy and, 77–78
>international law on, sources of, 31
>Islamic, themes of, 41–43
>Islamic opposition to Western standards of, 40–41
>Islamic views on, 41–43

among conservative scholars, 42–44

among liberal scholars, 45

Human Rights: Concepts and Standards (Symonides, ed.), 30

Human Rights in Islam (Mawdudi), 42, 43–44

Human Rights Internet, 120

Human Rights Watch, 12, 66, 109, 136, 139

Hussein, Saddam, 48, 50

In Larger Freedom (United Nations), 110

Integrated Regional Information Networks, 140

Inter-American Committee on Human Rights, 80

International Committee of the Red Cross (IRC), 68

    on detainment of children at Guantánamo, 75

International Court of Justice, 30

International Covenant on Civil and Political Rights (ICCPR), 17–25, 28–29, 105

International Covenant on Economic, Social and Cultural Rights (ICESCR), 28–29, 41, 105

International Criminal Court (ICC)

    Darfur and, 139, 140

    importance of, 152

    Internet and, 116

International Monetary Fund (IMF), 29

    involvement of, in human rights issues, 149–50

International Tribunal for Rwanda, 34

International Tribunal for the Former Yugoslavia, 34

Internet

    China's restrictions on, 87

    criminal use of, 115

    efforts to control, 115–17

    as human rights tool, 120–21

    spreading access to, 119

    as tool of democratization, 117–19

Iran, 14, 40, 50

    isolation of, 86

Israeli-Palestinian conflict, U.S. perceptions of, 147–48

Janjaweed militia, 64, 65, 66, 140

Jiang Zemin, 52, 137

Justice and Equity Movement (JEM), 63

Kalma camp (Darfur), 141–42

Kamminga, Menno, 100

Karimov, Islam, 47–49

Khomeini, Ayatollah Ruhollah, 42

Koh, Harold Hongju, 99

Kong Youping, 55

League of Nations, minority system under, 36, 37

Liberia, refugees from, 123, 124–26

    UNHCR screening of, 129–31

Li Dan, 53–54

Lowenkron, Barry, 85, 86, 87, 89

El-Mahdi, Sadij, 63

Malaysia, minority rights in, 83

Mao Zedong, 132

Mawdudi, Allamah Abu al'Ala, 42, 43–44

media

    global, exposes human rights abuses, 90

    independent, 79

        concentration in ownership of, 81

Mehta, Hansa, 104

Mertus, Julie A., 26

Middle East
  debate over human rights in, 40–41
  free trade and promotion of democracy in, 94

Millennium Development Goals (MDGs), 105–106
  role of NGOs in attainment of, 108–109

Millennium Summit (2000), 105, 106–107

minority rights
  in democracies, 82–84
  in early human rights conventions, 35–36
  in post-colonial Africa, 63

Moorehead, Caroline, 123

Murray, Craig, 48

Musharraf, Pervez, 87

Muslim Brotherhood, 51

"Muslim Commentary on the Universal Declaration of Human Rights" (Tabandeh), 41–42

Muslim Council, 42

Myanmar (Burma), Unocal and human rights abuses in, 98, 99

Al-Na'im, Abdullahi Ahmed, 45

National Islamic Front (NIF), 63

nationalism
  Islam and, 41
  protection of minority rights and, 37

nations, responsibility of, for human rights violations
  individual responsibility vs., 32–34
  unjust consequences of, 34–35

NATO (North Atlantic Treaty Organization), 28

New Economic Partnership for African Development (NEPAD), 149

New York Times (newspaper), 15, 69

NGOs. *See* nongovernmental organizations

nongovernmental organizations (NGOs)
  in developing countries, Internet training of, 119
  increased influence of, 103
  role in attainment of Millennium Development Goals, 108–109
  use of power of shame by, 79–80

Ocampo, Luis Moreno, 139

Okonkwo, Festus, 142

Optional Protocol to the Convention on the Rights of Children, 75

Organization of the Islamic Conference, 42

Organization on Security and Co-operation in Europe (OSCE), 36–37

Palestinian-Israeli conflict, U.S. perceptions of, 147–48

Peace and Security Council, 61

Peng-chung Chang, 104

politics
  religion and, in Islam, 42–43
  See also elections

poverty
  free trade reduces, 94
  human rights as framework for addressing, 149
  reduction strategies, UNHCR efforts in, 149
  in Sudan, 113

as violation of human dignity, 106

Pubantz, Jerry, 102

Qutb, Sayyid, 42

Ratner, Michael, 67
Redford, Katie, 97
Re-education Through Labour, 57, 151
refugees
    from Darfur crisis, 64
    Human Rights Commission as insult to, 113
    Liberian, in Egypt, 123
        UNHCR screening of, 129–30
    Uighur, 58
religion
    politics and, in Islam, 42–43
    repression of, in China, 55–56
rendition, 48, 89
Resolution 31, 109
Resolution 1473 (UN Security Council), 150
Rhode, David, 72
Rice, Condoleezza, 87
Robinson, Mary, 145
Roosevelt, Eleanor, 104–105
Roosevelt, Franklin D., 47
Rumsfeld, Donald, 48
    on Guantánamo detainees, 69
Russia, 15, 80, 115
    democratic backsliding in, 86, 88

Sahliyeh, Emile, 39
Santa Cruz, Hernán, 104
Sayed, Abassin, 70–71
Schrage, Elliot, 99, 100
Schulz, William F., 89
separation of powers, 79

September 11 attacks (2001), 67
    promotion of human rights-based development and, 28, 90
    regression on human rights as reaction to, 150–51
    U.S. acceptance of refugees following, 130
Serbia
    Internet use and elections in, 119
    see also Yugoslavia
Sharia (Islamic law), 42, 44
    reinterpretation of, 54
Sherif, Musa, 123–24, 126–29
"Sleepless in Sudan," 138
Somoza, Anastasio, 47
South Korea, economic reform in, 93
Sudan, 62
    genocide in, 86
    as member of UN Human Rights Commission, 112–13
    see also Darfur
Sudanese Liberation Army (SLA), 63, 138
Syria, 87–88

Tabandeh, Sultanhussain, 41, 42
Taiwan, economic reform in, 93
Taylor, Charles, 126
terrorism
    economic stagnation in Middle East promotes, 94
    in China, 57–58
    war against, U.S. human rights abuses and, 89
Tiananmen Square protest (1989), 134
torture
    of Afghan and Iraqi prisoners, 28
    in China, 56–57
    of Guantánamo detainees, 73

leads to false confessions, 74

outsourcing of, by U.S., 89

in Universal Declaration of Human Rights, 19

in Uzbekistan, 48

"Trading Tyranny for Freedom" (Cato Institute), 93

truth and reconciliation commissions, 84

for El Salvador, 34

Al-Turabj, 42

Turkey, reforms in, 13–14

Udombana, Nsongurua J., 59–60

Uighurs (ethnic community)

China's human rights violations against, 57–58

labeling of, as terrorists, 151

Um Gunya (Darfur), 140

UN Commission on Human Rights (CHR), 104

abusers of human rights on, 14

Annan on 2005 opening session of, 110

failure of US to vie for seat on, 13

human rights violators on, 14–15, 112–13

United Nations, 12, 17, 110

Darfur as challenge to, 60–61

democratization of, 103

human rights practice of, 27–29

move for human rights as issue for, 104–105

peacekeeping interventions by, 107–108

United Nations and Human Rights: A Guide for a New Era, The (Mertus), 26

United Nations Charter, 18, 31–32, 35

lack of clause establishing human rights in, 36

large-scale human rights violations and, 37–38

United Nations Development Programme (UNDP), 28

United Nations Educational, Scientific, and Cultural Organization (UNESCO), 116

United Nations Genocide Convention, 105

minority rights in, 35–36

United Nations High Commissioner for Human Rights (UNHCHR), 61, 62, 118

screening of refugees by, 129–31

United Nations High Commissioner for Refugees (UNHCR), 61, 127

United Nations International Covenant on Civil and Political Rights, 35

United Nations Security Council (UNSC), 60, 139, 146

actions taken against gross human rights violations, 37–38

Darfur and, 60

enlargement of, 110

United States

cutback on African Union funding by, 142

despots backed by, 50

foreign policy of

trade as tool of, 93

Uzbekistan and, 48–49

human rights violations by, 89

against Guantánamo detainees, 73, 75

perceptions of, on Israeli vs. Palestinian suffering, 147–48 rejection of International Criminal Court by, 152

Universal Declaration of Human Rights, 12, 17–25, 28–29, 41, 105

Guantánamo Bay prison and violations of, 67

minority rights in, 35

precursors to, 31

"Universal Islamic Declaration of Human Rights, The" (Muslim Council), 42

Unocal Corporation, 96–99

UN Office for the Coordination of Humanitarian Affairs, 140

UNSC. See United Nations Security Council

Uzbekistan, 14, 47, 88

response to protests in, 49, 88

torture methods used in, 48

Venezuela, 15, 86

censorship in, 88

Vienna Conference (World Conference on Human Rights), 106–107

violations of human rights

establishment of individual responsibility for, 32–35

by groups within states, 33

large-scale, UN authority to deal with, 37–38

lawsuits against corporations complicit in, 97–98

Bush administration's opposition to, 99

precedents for, 98

shift from governmental to individual responsibility for, 32–34

Wang Junying, 136

Wang Wanxing, 132–35

in Ankang system, 135–36

release of, 136–37

war, Islamic law on, 44

war crimes tribunals, individual responsibility established at, 33–34

Williams, Ian, 145

women

human rights violations against

in China, 54–55

in Darfur, 64

Internet as organizing tool for, 119

provisions for, in Universal Declaration of Human Rights, 23

World Bank, 29

involvement of, in human rights issues, 149–50

World Conference on Human Rights (Vienna Conference), 106–107

World Trade Organization (WTO), 94–95

involvement of, in human rights issues, 149–50

Youth International Internship Programme (YIIP), 119

Yugoslavia, minority rights violations in, 84

Zhou Enlai, 134

Zimbabwe

as member of UN Commission on Human Rights, 112–13

repression in, 88